Fodor's CITYPACK

MILAN'S
25 BEST

WITH FULL-SIZE
FOLDOUT MAP

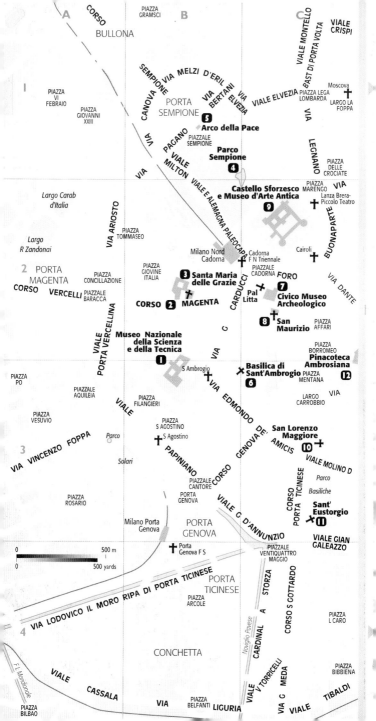

Top 25 locator map
(continues on inside
back cover)

←

Fodor's CITYPACK

MILAN'S **25** BEST

by Jackie Staddon
and Hilary Weston

Fodor's Travel Publications
New York • Toronto •
London • Sydney • Auckland
www.fodors.com

About This Book

KEY TO SYMBOLS

🕂 Map reference to the accompanying fold-out map and Top 25 locator map

✉ Address

☎ Telephone number

🕐 Opening/closing times

🍴 Restaurant or café on premises or nearby

🚆 Nearest railway station

Ⓜ Nearest subway (tube) station

🚌 Nearest bus route

⛴ Nearest riverboat or ferry stop

♿ Facilities for visitors with disabilities

💷 Admission charges: Expensive (over €6), Moderate (€3–6) and Inexpensive (under €3)

↔ Other nearby places of interest

❓ Other practical information

➤ Indicates the page where you will find a fuller description

ℹ Tourist information

ORGANIZATION

This guide is divided into six chapters:
- Planning Ahead, Getting There
- Living Milan–Milan Now, Milan Then, Time to Shop, Out and About, Walks, Milan by Night
- Milan's Top 25 Sights
- Milan's Best–best of the rest
- Where To–detailed listings of restaurants, hotels, shops and nightlife
- Travel Facts–practical information

In addition, easy-to-read side panels provide extra facts and snippets, highlights of places to visit and invaluable practical advice.

The colours of the tabs on the page corners match the colours of the triangles aligned with the chapter names on the contents page opposite.

MAPS

The fold-out map in the wallet at the back of this book is a comprehensive street plan of Milan. The first (or only) grid reference given for each attraction refers to this map. **The Top 25 locator map** found on the inside front and back covers of the book itself is for quick reference. It shows the Top 25 Sights, described on pages 26–50, which are clearly plotted by number (**1**–**25**, not page number) in the authors' suggested viewing order. The second map reference given for the Top 25 Sights refers to this map.

Contents

Planning Ahead

WHEN TO GO

Milan is primarily a business destination so there is not much seasonal variation in the number of visitors or cost of hotels, but avoid visiting during major events, such as fashion shows. April, May, June and September are good months to visit. Temperatures start to climb in June, and to dip again at the end of September when there are increasing bouts of rain.

TIME

Italy is one hour ahead of GMT, six hours ahead of New York and nine hours ahead of Los Angeles.

AVERAGE DAILY MAXIMUM TEMPERATURES

JAN	FEB	MAR	APR	MAY	JUN	JUL	AUG	SEP	OCT	NOV	DEC
43°F	46°F	54°F	59°F	68°F	73°F	79°F	79°F	70°F	61°F	54°F	45°F
6°C	8°C	12°C	15°C	20°C	23°C	26°C	26°C	21°C	16°C	12°C	7°C

Spring (March to May) is very pleasant, although rain can persist into May.
Summer (June to August) high temperatures bring a humid haze and normally some thunderstorms, which help to clear the air.
Autumn (September to November) gradually turns from showers to heavy rain, and November is dank and wet.
Winter (December to February) Alpine winds make it very cold and there can be heavy frosts and thick fog. December can produce pleasant bright, crisp days.

WHAT'S ON

January *Corteo dei Re Magi* (6 Jan): A Nativity themed procession travels from the Duomo to Sant'Eustorgio.
February *Carnevale Ambrosiano*: The carnival culminates with a parade on the first Saturday of Lent.
March *MODIT-Milanovendemodo* (early Mar): International fashion show.
Milano–SanRemo (third Sat): Milan hosts the start of this famous international bicycle race.
April *Fiera dei Fiori* (Mon after Easter): Fair devoted to flower growing, near the Sant'Angelo Franciscan convent.
Stramilano (early-Apr): Annual marathon race with over 50,000 competitors.
June *Festa del Naviglio* (first Sun): Festival held along the Navigli canals; concerts, street performers, sports, handicrafts and regional cooking.
July/August *Festival Latino-Americano*: Festival of Latin-American music, handicrafts and cuisine.
September *Gran Premio di Monza*: Formula One Grand Prix of Italy.
October *MODIT-Milanovendemoda* (early Oct): second major fashion show.
December *Mercato di Sant'Ambrogio* (7 Dec): Festival in honour of Sant'Ambrogio, Milan's 4th-century patron saint and the city's first mayor. Stalls are set up around the church of Sant'Ambrogio and most people take the day off work to attend the market. Also called Oh Bej! Oh Bej! after the children's cries of delight in the 16th century.

MILAN ONLINE
www.milaninfotourist.com
Milan's official website includes practical information on city sights, accommodation, restaurants, entertainment, events, guided tours, transportation and lots more. Updated regularly.

www.hellomilano.it
English site that is easy to understand and has good up-to-date details on what's on, news, restaurants, nightlife, shopping and general information.

www.enit.it
The main Italian Tourist Board website carries a wealth of information about the whole country—available in several languages.

www.emmeti.it
An Italy-based site, in English and Italian, with a good range of information on Milan and links to other sites. It's strong on local events and offers an online hotel booking service.

www.initaly.com
An enthusiastic site run by passionate lovers of Italy from the US. It's packed with information and articles about the country, with quirky tips and insider stories, and makes excellent browsing when you're planning your trip.

www.hotelme.it
A user-friendly hotel booking service, with good coverage of Milan. Previous visitors share opinions and tips. English version available.

www.ticketweb.it
Buy your tickets for nearly every event going on in Milan—theatre, music, sport, exhibitions.

**www.apt.pavia.it/www.aptcremona.it/
www.apt.bergamo**
Official website of the Azienda di Promozione Turistica (APT) offices for Pavia, Cremona and Bergamo. All have English versions and provide comprehensive information.

PRIME TRAVEL SITES

www.atm-mi.it
Milan's city transport system runs this informative site, where you'll find everything you could possibly want to know, including timetables, maps and how to buy the best ticket for your needs—Italian and English.

www.trenitalia.it
The official site of the Italian State Railways with excellent train information and a user-friendly search facility—good for forward planning.

CYBERCAFÉS

Gr@zianet
Large café with plenty of computers just outside Stazione Centrale.
✉ Piazza Duca d'Aosta 14, 20124 ☎ 02 670 0543
🕐 Daily 8am–2am 🖐 €4 per hour

Mondadori
Inside Mondadori Multicentre—a music, book and software megastore.
✉ Via Marghera 28, 20129 ☎ 02 2953 6270
🕐 Mon 1–7.30, Tue–Fri 10–1, 2–7.30, Sat 10–2, 3–7.30 🖐 €2 per hour

Getting There

ENTRY REQUIREMENTS

All visitors to Italy require a valid passport. Visas may not be required by UK, US, Canadian, Australian, New Zealand or Irish citizens, or other EU nationals staying less than three months—check with the Embassy in your home country before leaving. Health and accident insurance is strongly recommended.

ARRIVING

There are direct flights from all over the world into Malpensa airport, Milan's main international gateway, while Linate airport, classed as a city airport, handles just Italian domestic and European flights. Visitors from Europe can also arrive by rail or by bus.

✈ Malpensa

52km (32 miles)   26km (16 miles)   13km (8 miles)   **Milan**   ✈ Linate

MONEY

The euro (€) is the official currency of Italy. Banknotes are in denominations of 5, 10, 20, 50, 100, 200 and 500 euros, and coins in denominations of 1, 2, 5, 10, 20, 50 cents and 1 and 2 euros.

€50

€200

€500

FROM MALPENSA

Most flights arrive at Malpensa, 50km (31 miles) northwest of the city. The Malpensa Express train runs to Cadorna–Ferrovie Nord (every 30 minutes, 6am–1.30am; €9, journey time 45–50 minutes). The Malpensa Bus Express leaves from outside the terminal to Stazione Centrale (every 20 minutes, 5.10am–10.30pm; €5.50, journey time 50–60 minutes). Bus Air Pullman operates a shuttle bus to Stazione Centrale (every 20 minutes, 5.20am–10.30pm; €4.50, journey time 50–60 minutes). Taxis to the city can take up to an hour depending on the traffic and are expensive (€60–75).

FROM LINATE

Linate is only 6km (4 miles) east of the city. The most convenient option for getting into the city is by taxi; official white cabs line up outside the terminal (€20–25, but check the cost before). ATM city bus No. 73 (every 20 minutes, 5.30am–12.20am) goes to Piazza San Babila (tickets €1 from vending machines). Bus Starfly run a service to Stazione Centrale (every 30 minutes, 6.05am–11.35pm; €2.50).

Arriving by Rail
Most international and domestic trains arrive at Stazione Centrale, northeast of the city. There are easy connections to the rest of the city from here: The station is on Metro lines 2 and 3, taxis line up outside the entrance, and several trams and buses stop right outside.

Arriving by Bus
The majority of domestic and international buses arrive at the main terminus in Piazza Castello. Autostradale Viaggi is the major bus company connecting Milan with the rest of Italy.

Getting Around
Milan has an efficient integrated transportation system comprising trams, buses and a Metro, which is easy to use. The Metro is the easiest and fastest option, though you may have to combine it with a bus or tram. The Metro consists of four lines: red MM1, green MM2, yellow MM3 and blue *passante ferroviario*. These intersect at the hub stations of Stazione Centrale, Duomo, Cardorna and Loreto. Bus and tram routes cover the whole city and also follow the Metro routes overground.

Tickets must be purchased in advance and stamped in a machine once on board. Fines are handed out to anyone caught without a ticket. A single (€1.15) is valid for 75 minutes from validation and can be used on the entire system for as many bus and tram trips as you want, plus one Metro journey. One- and two-day travel cards are also available. Tickets are sold at tobacconists, bars, news-stands, APT offices and Metro stations. The network runs 6am–midnight, with night buses continuing until 1.30am.

Official taxis in Milan are normally white and the charges are reasonable. It is difficult to hail a passing cab so it's best to call (Radiotaxi ☎ 02 4040; 02 8585; 02 8383) when you want one—they usually arrive quite quickly—or go to a taxi rank (stand) at Piazza del Duomo, Stazione Centrale, Piazza della Scala, Piazza San Babila, Piazza Diaz and Via Manzoni.

HANDY HINT

In the land of the Vespa, it's tempting to hire a scooter (*motorino*) and Milan has many scooter rental outlets. But scooters are not for the faint-hearted, and if you've never ridden one in a big city, Milan is not the place to start.

VISITORS WITH DISABILITIES

Milan is rapidly upgrading its facilities for visitors with disabilities. Many hotels and restaurants are accessible and the situation is improving in museums and monuments all the time. A growing number of buses have ramps or lower floors for wheelchair users and some underground trains are wheelchair-friendly: look for the logo on the side of the train. The AIAS organization in Milan, provides in-depth details of access for specific hotels, restaurants and the main tourist sights, plus information about public transport. Their website is also in English.

AIAS Milano
www.milanopertutti.it
✉ Via Mittadini 3
☎ 02 330 2021

Living
Milan

Milan Now

Above: Street musicians add to the city's atmosphere
Centre top: The Milanese look stylish, even when sightseeing
Centre bottom: One of the statues on the façade of Casa Fontana Silvestri

Milan is not all it appears. This is a city of contrasts and hidden depths. Its reputation is one of commercialism driven by market forces, and indeed it is the powerhouse of Italy's economy. There are major companies representing all branches of industry, big banks and Italy's Stock Exchange. Milan boasts huge trade fairs and exhibitions, catwalk extravaganzas and celebrity status, and is home to two of the top European football teams—AC Milan and Inter Milan. Here you can indulge in some of the best designer shopping in Europe, not just for fashion but for interior design, too.

DISTRICTS

• Milan is divided into 20 named zones, each with its own particular history and identity. Most visitors will probably only visit those within a few Metro stops of the Duomo area. Moving out from the *centro storico* around the Piazza Duomo, the principal areas are: to the north, the attractive old Brera district with its winding streets that still retain their 18th-century paving; to the northeast, the famous fashion streets that lead to the Giardini Pubblici and the Stazione Centrale; to the northwest, the Castello Sforzesco and the Parco Sempione; and to the south, Ticinese, an up-and-coming shopping area, and the Navigli, once a hive of commercial activity and now a gentrified area with antique shops, cafés, bars and traditional trattorias.

Above: Around the city on two wheels
Left: Castello Sforzesco

LEONARDO'S HORSE

● The largest bronze equine statue in the world at 7m (24ft) high, this is a replica of a monument that Leonardo da Vinci was commissioned to build in 1482. However, it didn't get beyond model stage, and was finally cast in 1999 in the US. It rather appropriately stands outside the horse-racing stadium, the Ippodrome (► 85) in San Siro.

Although Milan does not depend on tourism to survive, the city does have lots to offer those looking for a break. It may seem to lack the charm of other Italian cities and towns, but if you scratch beneath the surface you will find it has its own unique personality. Its geographical location means it has traditionally looked north and has more in common with the northern Europeans than its southern cousins. It does not attract the hoards of tourists that flock to Rome, Florence and Venice, and while it does have a lot of traffic and rush hour congestion, the city is a comfortable place to live and visit, and exudes a sense of well being. The Milanese are happy in their own skin, unruffled and confident—busy,

Above: Feeding the pigeons at Piazza Duomo

yes, but they always find time to be sociable and polite.

Despite suffering considerable damage from heavy bombing during World War II, Milan spearheaded Italy's post-war economic recovery by re-establishing its heavy industry. This was followed by a move into the high-tech industries and an increase in the banking sector. The city suffered from huge immigration problems in the 1980s and in the 1990s with bribery, corruption and political intrigues. The current Prime Minister, Silvio Berlusconi, himself a native of Milan and a self-made businessman, was also caught up in these political scandals.

Milan is not just about commercialism and business, it has a strong sense of history and tradition. The Duomo is an extraordinary piece of architecture (► 43) set in the historic heart of the city. Milan has some of the finest churches in

MILAN FOR FREE

• There are many free museums in Milan and churches do not charge for entry, although there may be a small fee to see a specific painting. The Castello Sforzesco and the surrounding Parco Sempione are also free. Wandering the attractive canal district and the old artist quarter of Brera, or window-shopping in the designer streets won't cost anything either— that's if you can resist temptation.

Above: The columns at Colonne di San Lorenzo

Italy, and many ordinary shopping or office streets have architectural gems concealed behind the modern exteriors. There are numerous beautiful palazzos as well, imposing and proud reminders of Milan's aristocratic past. The many well-run museums offer a glimpse into the city's fine artistic and historic heritage. For art and music lovers Milan has few equals. This is the home of the great La Scala opera house and the famous *Last Supper* painted by

MILAN FACTS

- Milan's land area covers 181.7sq km (70sq miles)
- The population of Milan is 1.3 million (Greater Milan: 4 million)
- The Duomo is the third largest church in the world
- Milan is home to Italy's Stock Exchange, La Borsa
- La Scala has one of the world's largest stages at 1,200sq m/13,000sq ft.
- Trade fairs in Milan draw over 4 million visitors per year
- Milan's most important art treasure is *The Last Supper* painted by Leonardo da Vinci who lived in Milan from 1482–1499

TRADE FAIRS

- Apart from the months of July and August, there is a trade fair occurring virtually every week in Milan. These are nearly all held at the Fiera di Milano, which covers a vast area with some 26 pavilions hosting international fairs, the most prominent being those concerned with fashion and interior design.

Above: Join the Milanese,
and drink your coffee
standing up at the bar
Above right: The soaring
pinacles of the Duomo

MILAN'S SKYSCRAPERS

• The most famous of these is the Pirelli building (➤ 60), which remains one of the symbols of Milan. It is the highest at 127m (417ft) and is followed closely by the Milan skyscraper at 114m (374ft), the Galfa building at 104m (341ft) and the Velasca Tower at 99m (325ft).

Leonardo da Vinci. The major sights are all within easy walking distance of the *centro storico*, with trams and the Metro linking other places of interest farther afield. The city could never be described as green but, if you explore, you will discover pretty parks and hidden gardens that act as tranquil oases from the hustle and bustle.

Public transportation is excellent: efficient, clean and reasonably priced. The Metro system is reliable and for places that you can't reach by underground, the trams and buses offer a good, if slower, alternative. Unlike some other Italian cities, the Milanese don't make excessive use of their car horns, giving the city a more relaxed, polite air.

Shopaholics will, without doubt, have a field day in Milan. There is fantastic shopping at every level from the ultra-chic designer stores to atmospheric street markets. Even if you can't afford the often-exorbitant prices, it is still worth wandering the streets of the Quadrilatero d'Oro to see the magnificent window displays or observe glitzy customers buying the latest

fashion must-have. The style doesn't stop with clothing—even the humblest delicatessens have a certain flair with their displays.

Just beyond the *centro storico* there are other fascinating districts with a totally different feel, like the Brera, which has some excellent shopping options and a variety of interesting restaurants, or the Navigli where renovation is rejuvenating the area, filling it with antique shops, clubs and bars while still retaining the traditional *osterie*.

Milan combines the best of both worlds: on the one hand it is grandiose, with its fine theatres and elaborate church frescoes, but on the other, the simpler Italian lifestyle has not been totally rejected. Despite their modern approach to business and their trendy get-up-and-go ways they still cling to the traditional—comforting wood-panelled historic cafés and family-run *trattorias*. There's an old adage, 'Milan l'è Milan'—Milan is just Milan. And though the city may not have the beauty of Florence, the grandeur of Rome or the romance of Venice, it does have a diversity that is very appealing.

SOCCER CRAZY

● Many Milanese take more pride in the city's world-class soccer teams, Inter and AC Milan, than its economic and historic heritage, and on match days, the San Siro stadium is crammed with over 85,000 supporters. Obsessive hero-worship of past stars such as AC's Cesare Maldini has passed to present day players like his son, Paulo. Italian children are born and bred on soccer, and in Milan's parks you can see youngsters kicking a ball, dreaming of becoming the next Maldini.

15

Milan Then

*Above: A sculpted portal
from the Duomo
Above right: An engraving of
Milan's Duomo*

EARLY BEGINNINGS

During the Bronze Age,
the Ligurians were the
first to settle in the Po
Valley, and by the sixth
century BC the powerful
Etruscans were well
ensconced. By 338–386BC,
after various skirmishes,
the area was ruled by
the Gauls.

SANT'AMBROGIO

The patron saint of Milan,
whose feast day is on 7
December, was Bishop of
Milan from AD374–397. As
a result of his integrity
and skill in negotiating
between the Catholic and
Arian church officials,
Milan became an
important religious hub.

222BC The Romans defeat the Gauls. Milan becomes the most important city in the Western Roman Empire after Rome.

AD374 Sant'Ambrogio (St. Ambrose) becomes Bishop of Milan. The city flourishes.

452 The city is devastated by Attila the Hun, then again in 489 by the Goths.

568 Lombards invade and take power.

774 Rebirth of the city under the rule of Charlemagne.

1042 Milan becomes an autonomous city.

1162 German Emperor Frederick I invades. Milan is burned to the ground.

1176 Battle of Legnano gives independence to northern Italian cities.

1277 Rise of the Visconti family with Gian Galeazzo Visconti becoming the first Duke of Milan in 1395. The Duomo is commissioned in 1386.

1450 Rise of the Sforza family; for 50 years art and commerce flourish.

1499 Louis XII of France occupies Milan.

1540–
1706 Milan under Spanish rule.

1630 Plague reduces the population to 60,000.

1706 Control of the city passes to the Austrian Habsburgs.

1796– Napoleonic rule. New building work
1814 is undertaken.

1804 Napoleon's coronation at the Duomo.

1815 Napoleon is defeated and Milan is handed back to the Habsburgs.

1848 Unification—Milan becomes part of Italy. The population increases to 240,000.

1919 Fascist movement founded by Benito Mussolini in Milan.

1939– Milan suffers serious bomb damage
1945 during World War II.

1950s Milan leads Italy's economic recovery.

1960s Industrial and student unrest. Acts of terrorism take place.

1990s Corruption and political scandal rife; Milan becomes known as 'bribe' city.

2002 The euro becomes the official currency of Italy.

2004 La Scala opens after 3 years of closure for restoration.

NAPOLEON'S RULE

The city of Milan welcomed the arrival of Napoleon, and indeed it was he who brought forward the idea of the unification of Italy. His contributions to the city included reforming the educational and legal system, inaugurating the building of new public offices and establishing new museums and art galleries. He even saw the completion of the Duomo so he could hold his coronation there as the self-appointed 'king of Italy'. However, after 18 years of rule and high taxation the Milanese people were relieved when Napoleon was defeated at the Battle of Waterloo and Milan was returned to Habsburg rule.

17

Time to Shop

Shoes by Italian designer, Valentino

Said to be the world's design capital, a visit to Milan's sensational fashion district is high on many visitors' itinerary, and designer clothes can be cheaper here than in New York or London.

PANETTONE

This famous Milanese cake, made with eggs, flour, sugar, candied fruits and spices, is now served at Christmas throughout Italy. It is said to have originated in the 15th century when the dessert at the Christmas Eve banquet for Ludovico Sforza was burned. It was rescued by Toni, a kitchen boy, who salvaged the remains of the burnt cake and added new ingredients. Since that day 'pan del Toni' became known as *panettone* and has remained popular ever since.

Milan's most popular shopping area for *haute couture* is without doubt the network of pretty streets known as The Golden Triangle, bordered by Via Montenapoleone, Via Manzoni, Via Sant'Andrea and Via Spiga. Here you will find designer clothes, accessories, shoes and leatherwear presented in chic, minimalist interiors that are works of art themselves. Even when the shops are closed the streets are full of visitors admiring the window displays.

You can also shop for superior goods at the glass-domed Galleria Vittorio Emanuele II (► 44); the slightly bohemian Corso di Porta Ticinese, where there are smaller, trendy boutiques; or the up-and-coming Isola area with some interesting boutiques. There are plenty of less elitist stores selling more affordable items around Corso Vittorio Emanuele II, Via Torino, Corsa di Porta Romana and Corso Buenos Aires. Milan is also at the forefront of interior design, from the elegant to the wacky. Large ultra-modern showrooms stocked with original trend-setting items are apparent throughout the city. Smaller items that can be easily taken home include kitchen gadgets, decorated glass and sleek, stylish lighting.

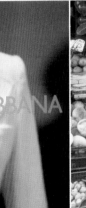

Centre: Dolce & Gabbana are just one of the designer names you'll find in Milan Left: Fresh produce is sold in every district of the city

If you are looking for some traditionally Milanese products to take home, try some *panettone* (see panel opposite) or pick up a bottle of fine Italian wine from a reputable *enoteche*, where every purchase is beautifully wrapped. For that special gift, head to one of the delightful stationery shops that stock handcrafted paper-based products. The items are produced using luxury paper, hand-made from such materials as silk, coconut, lace and bamboo, in every hue and shade.

Antiques enthusiasts will enjoy browsing in the numerous antique shops around the Brera district and along the canals, where regular antique markets (➤ 79) are held. Shops specializing in old and new prints and lithographs, art galleries and auction houses are plentiful in Milan. For book lovers, the city has more than its fair share of spacious well-stocked bookshops, some selling books in many languages. There are also smaller, specialist bookshops that stock rare or out-of-print books.

FACTORY OUTLETS

If you are unable to pay the high prices of Milan's fashion district, don't despair. Factory outlets, stores that offer last season's products at a fraction of the price, are becoming very popular in Milan. Although, as the city has a reputation to uphold as one of the world's most important fashion hubs, many of the biggest designers are reluctant to put their name to outlet stores because they don't wish to be seen selling their creations at discount prices. You can also pick up sensational bargains during the end of season sales (January/February or July/August).

19

Out and About

Below: The Contarini
Fountain in Bergamo
Below right: Visitors and
worshippers in Cremona

BERGAMO

Distance 48km (30 miles)
Time 1 hour
🚊 Regular service from
Garibaldi FS
Tourist Information
www.apt.bergamo.it
✉ Viale Vittorio Emanuele
20 ☎ 035 210 204

Basilica of Santa Maria Maggiore
✉ Piazza Duomo
☎ 035 223 327
🕐 Apr–end Oct daily
9–12.30, 2.30–6; Nov–end
Mar Mon–Sat 9–12.30,
2.30–5, Sun 9–1, 3–6
🎟 Free

Cappella Colleoni
✉ Piazza Duomo
☎ 035 210 061
🕐 Mar–end Oct Tue–Sun
9–12.30, 2.30–6.30;
Nov–end Feb Tue–Sun
9–12.30, 2–4.30
🎟 Free

Accademia Carrara
✉ Piazza dell'Accademia
☎ 035 399 643
🕐 Apr–end Sep Tue–Sun
10–1, 3–6.45; Oct–end
Mar Tue–Sun 9.30–1,
2.30–5.45
🎟 Inexpensive

ORGANIZED SIGHTSEEING

A bus tour leaves Piazza Duomo (Tue–Sun
9.30am) for a 3-hour tour to most of Milan's
main sights, accompanied by a multilingual
commentary; cost €42 including pick up and
drop off at selected hotel and entrance fees. For
a fascinating overview of the city take the Tram

Turistico—a hop-on hop-off guided tour with
multilingual recorded commentary aboard a
1920s tram. It departs from Piazza Castello
(Apr–Oct daily 11, 1, 3; winter Sat and holidays
only) and lasts for about 1 hour 45 minutes;
cost €20. You can buy tickets for both tours at
the APT offices or call ☎ 02 3391 0794.

An alternative is to view the city on foot. Tourist
Guide of Milan (Via Marconi 1 ☎ 02 8645 0433)
offers themed tours by expert guides. A Friend in
Milan (☎ 02 2952 0570) is another organization
that provides guided walking tours throughout
the city.

EXCURSIONS
BERGAMO
Remarkably unspoiled, historic Bergamo crowns
a steep hill. The city is divided into the medieval
Città Alta (Upper Town), within 16th-century
walls, and the contrasting modern, traffic-filled
Città Bassa (Lower Town). A funicular transports
you to *Città Alta* and its picturesque cobbled
alleyways and medieval and Renaissance

buildings. Visit Piazza del Duomo, where the Duomo pales against the Renaissance porch of the Basilica of Santa Maria Maggiore and lavish facade of the Cappella Colleoni. The highlight of the lower town is the Galleria Accademia Carrara and its collection of Venetian, Bergamesque and other works of art.

PAVIA
Pavia is graced by fine Romanesque and medieval buildings, but what really draws the crowds is the nearby 14th-century monastery, Certosa di Pavia (8km/5 miles north of Pavia). This is one of the most extravagant religious complexes in Northern Italy—the exuberant façade in multitoned marble has a wealth of inlay and sculpture. Inside there is a profusion of Renaissance and baroque art.

CREMONA
A quiet market town on the banks of the River Po, Cremona has been the heart of the violin-making industry since 1566. The greatest violin maker, Antonio Stradivari, was born here in 1644, and is commemorated in the Museo Stradivariano. In the middle of town is Piazza del Comune, a fine medieval square with beautiful medieval monuments: the highest bell tower in Italy, the Romanesque/Gothic cathedral, the octagonal Baptistery (1167) and the Palazzo del Comune (1206–45). The Palazzo Comune has a collection of historic violins.

PAVIA

Distance 39km (24 miles)
Time 45 minutes
Famagosta station, then 15 min walk
Tourist Information
www.apt.pavia.it
Via Fabio Filzi 2
0382 22156

Certosa di Pavia
Viale del Monumento
Tue–Sun 9–11.30, 2.30–4.30
0382 925 613
Free (donations)

Castello Visconteo and Museo Civico
Piazza Castello
0382 33853/304816
Mar–end Jun, Sep–end Nov Tue–Fri 9–1.30, Sat and Sun 10–7; Jul–end Aug, Dec–end Feb Tue–Sat 9–1.30, Sun 9–1
Moderate

CREMONA

Distance 93km (58 miles)
Time 2 hours
Regular service from Centrale FS
Tourist Information
www.aptcremona.it
Piazza del Comune 5
0372 23233

Museo Stradivariano
Via Ugolani Dati
0372 407 770
Tue–Sat 9–6, Sun 10–7
Expensive

21

Walks

Distance 2km (1.25 miles)
Time 30–40 mins
(without stops), 2 hrs
plus with stops
🚇 Duomo
🚋 Tram 1, 2, 3, 12, 14, 24
and more
🍽 Ristorante al Mercante
☎ 02 805 2198 (➤ 65)

*Statue of Leonardo da Vinci
outside La Scala*

CITY HIGHLIGHTS

This stroll through the heart of Milan will introduce you to some of the city's most famous landmarks. On the way, you may be enticed to stop and shop, or sit at a café and watch the elegant world go by.

Start in the Piazza del Duomo, dominated by the west front of the magnificent late Gothic cathedral. In the middle of the Piazza is Ercole Rosa's bronze equestrian statue of Vittorio Emanuele II (1896). Walk along the right side of the Duomo (➤ 43), then turn right down the narrow Via Palazzo Reale, between Palazzo Reale and Palazzo Arcivescovile. Go round the back of the palace, via the lovely bell tower of St. Gottardo in Corte and the Pilgrims Rotunda. Turn left at the end of Via delle Ore for Piazza Fontana, where you will find the fountain designed by Piermarini in 1783. Look behind the fountain for a fine view of the Duomo.

Returning to the Piazza del Duomo, turn right through Galleria Vittorio Emanuele II (➤ 44) into Piazza della Scala, cross in front of the Palazzo Marino and turn right. Another immediate right behind the palazzo brings you into Piazza San Fedele with its baroque church and statue of writer Alessandro Manzoni. Leaving the piazza the way you entered, walk alongside the church until you see Casa degli Omenoni ahead on the left, home to the Mannerist sculptor Leone Leoni. Piazza Belgioioso beyond was named after the huge 18th-century palace of the Belgioioso d'Este family. Manzoni's house, at the end on the left, is now a museum. Continue to Via Manzoni. On your right is the charming Museo Poldi Pezzoli (➤ 45). Turn left back into Piazza della Scala with the opera house on your right.

Passing in front of La Scala, follow Via Santa Margherita down to Piazza Mercanti (➤ 39). In this old market square is the medieval arcaded Palazzo della Ragione, built in 1233.

Via Mercanti leads back to the Duomo.

SOME MILANESE TREASURES

Start at the clock tower entrance of the Castello Sforzesco (➤ 34). With your back to the castle, follow Piazza Castello around to the right and take the first left, Via Minghetti down Via G. Carducci to Piazzale Cadorna. Continue straight on until the road meets Corso Magenta, one of Milan's most elegant streets with its chic shops and historic palaces. Turn right into Magenta and follow this street until you reach the splendid church of Santa Maria delle Grazie with its magnificent brick and terracotta exterior. Here you may wish to pause to view Leonardo's *Last Supper* (➤ 28), which is in the adjoining Refectory, but be warned, it is often crowded.

Take Via B. Zenale diagonally opposite the church and continue down to Via San Vittore. Shortly afterwards on the right is the Museo Naxionale della Scienza e della Tecnica (➤ 26) with its excellent collection ranging from a full-size jet and fully rigged ship to the intriguing exhibition of Leonardo's inventions, where you can even activate some of his prototypes.

Continue east down Via San Vittore until you reach the junction with Via G. Carducci and Via Olona. Across the road in Piazza Sant'Ambrogio you can see the two bell towers of the striking Basilica di Sant'Ambrogio (➤ 31), a supreme example of Romanesque architecture. With the basilica to your left, continue along Via Santa Valeria and at the junction with Via Cappuccio turn left into Via Luini. At the end of Via Luini, as you reach Corso Magenta, you will find the church of San Maurizio, whose grey façade belies its glorious interior. Next door is the Civico Museo Archaeologico, with its wealth of Roman remains. Across the Corso Magenta is the Palazzo Litta (not open to the public), whose majestic façade dominates this part of the street. Continue west past the palace and then turn up the small street Via San Nicolao. This will lead you back to the Piazzale Cadorna where you can retrace your steps to the castle.

INFORMATION

Distance 3km (2 miles)
Time 1 hr, more with stops
Start/end point Castello Sforzesco
🚇 Cairoli, Cadorna
🚌 50, 58, 61, 70; tram 1, 3, 4, 12, 14, 27
🍴 Bindi (➤ 70)

Although austere on the outside, Santa Maria delle Grazie houses one of Milan's greatest treasures

Milan by Night

Above: Milan's Gothic cathedral
Above right: Piazza della Scala

After-hours entertainment in cosmopolitan Milan is vibrant. The city is known for Italy's hippest nightlife, with every type of entertainment. For those who prefer a slower pace, the city offers world-class opera, ballet and a theatre season that is the best and most varied in Italy. For the more energetic, there are glitzy nightclubs, trendy bars, disco pubs, lively cafés and live music venues.

None of this is evident until after dark when Milan's partygoers come out to play, and the streets are thronged with beautiful people. Evenings usually begin slowly with the *passeggiata*, a cultural institution in Italy, where everyone struts up and down the central streets, mainly around Galleria Vittorio Emanuele II and the pedestrian zones along Via Dante. As the pace picks up, two of the most popular areas to visit are the Navigli or canal area, which is bisected by pretty waterways and dotted with *osterie*, jazz bars and clubs, and the atmospheric Brera district, with intimate cafés, restaurants and clubs in its narrow cobbled streets.

Opera fans will want to attend a performance at La Scala, Milan's famous opera house. The season runs from December through to July, but performances sell out fast. There are many other places to enjoy classical music around the city, as well as live theatre, cultural events and a wide repertoire of plays. Then there are the city's many cinemas—several of them multiplexes—where the new releases are often shown ahead of most other Italian cities.

DISCOPUBS

Milan has a breed of pub popular with those who want to dance without being plunged into the noise and flashing lights of a full-blown disco; these are known as discopubs. Discopubs are ideal if you prefer to start the evening with a relaxing drink and quiet conversation, slowly building up to a party mood. Later into the evening the volume is turned up and the pub really starts to swing as every available space is taken up by disco divas performing the latest dance moves.

MILAN's
top 25 sights

The sights are shown on the maps on the inside front cover and inside back cover, numbered **1** – **25** in the authors' suggested viewing order

Museo Nazionale della Scienza e della Tecnica

HIGHLIGHTS

- Leonardo Gallery
- Leonardo self-portrait
- Watchmaker's workshop (1750)
- Early steam locomotives
- The *Ebe*, a huge schooner
- The *Conte Biancammo* a 1925 transatlantic liner with period furnishings
- Early computers

INFORMATION

www.museoscienza.org

✚ B2

✉ Via San Vittore 21, 20123

☎ 02 485 551

🕐 Tue–Fri 9.30–4.50, Sat–Sun, public hols 9.30–6.20

🍴 Self-service canteen noon–2; coffee bar same hours as museum

Ⓢ Sant'Ambrogio

🚌 50, 58, 94

♿ Good

💲 Expensive

↔ Corso Magenta (➤ 27), Santa Maria delle Grazie (➤ 28), Baslica di Sant'Ambrogio (➤ 31)

❓ Guided tours every Sun from mid-Jun to early Sep; free English tour with emphasis on the Leonardo section

This is one of the world's largest science and technology museums, with around 15,000 scientific exhibits and displays as diverse as arts and crafts and the workings of the internet.

Early beginnings The oldest of the three museum buildings is the Monastery of the Olivetani, founded in the 11th century and rebuilt in the 16th. Although much has been altered it still has two beautiful cloisters. The site became a military hospital and barracks under Napoleon and suffered heavy bomb damage in 1943. Restored for use as a museum, it opened in 1953 with an exhibition on Leonardo, to coincide with the fifth centenary of his birth.

Vast collections The labyrinthine museum is divided into 28 different sections with most of the scientific exhibits displayed at ground level, on the first floor and in the basement of this monumental building. The Civico Museo Navale Didattico, with an impressive collection of model ships and figureheads, is incorporated into the museum. There are also two separate buildings, devoted to rail, air and sea transport. Steam and electric trains are in the reconstructed art nouveau station, and aircraft and large ships can be found in the Air and Sea Transport building.

Planning your visit This museum can appear vast and daunting the first time you visit and you will need a lot of time to orientate yourself. Decide what you most want to see before your visit. The Leonardo Gallery is fascinating, though most of the explanations are in Italian only. If you take children, its best to head for the huge boats, steam trains, aircraft and hands-on playgrounds.

Corso Magenta

Any visit to Milan should include this corso, one of Milan's most elegant streets flanked by historic palazzi and home to Leonardo's *The Last Supper* at the Church of Santa Maria delle Grazie.

Along the old road The oldest trace of civilization here is the Roman tower in the grounds of the Archaeological Museum (▶ 32), the only surviving above-ground section of the city's Roman walls. On the same site are the ruins of the ancient Benedictine Maggiore Monastery, founded in the ninth century and remodelled in the early 1500s. The rest of Corso Magenta is more recent, typified by baroque, neoclassical and 19th-century mansions.

Plenty to see This is one of Milan's most affluent districts, a desirable residential and shopping area, with chic boutiques, antique shops and several historic buildings. The great magnet is the Church of Santa Maria delle Grazie whose splendid terracotta bulk dominates this section of the Corso. The piazza is normally milling with visitors, awaiting their alloted 15-minute slot for Leonardo's *The Last Supper* in the Refectory adjoining the church. While he was working on the painting, Leonardo stayed at 65 Palazzo Busca. This palace, which is just past Santa Maria and incorporates the remains of the Atellani residence, was decorated by Luini. Going east, the Palazzo delle Stelline at No. 59, a school for orphans in the 17th century, has been transformed out of recognition into a conference facility and hotel. Beyond the crossroads, you can't miss the large baroque façade of Palazzo Litta (No. 24: ▶ 57), and across the road, beyond the Archaeological Museum, the Church of San Maurizio (No. 15) is full of fabulous 16th-century frescoes.

HIGHLIGHTS

● Santa Maria delle Grazie and Leonardo's *Last Supper* (c.1495–97) (▶ 28)
● Museo Archeologico (▶ 32)
● San Maurizio (▶ 33)
● Museo Tetrale alla Scala (▶ 39)
● Bar Magenta–historic café

INFORMATION

✚ B2
✉ Extending east from Porta Magenta to the junction with Via Meravigli
🍴 Numerous cafés and restaurants
Ⓜ Conciliazione, Cadorna
🚊 18, 67; tram 16, 19
↔ Santa Maria delle Grazie (▶ 28), Museo Archeologico (▶ 32), San Maurizio (▶ 33)

27

Santa Maria delle Grazie

HIGHLIGHTS

- *Last Supper*, Leonardo da Vinci (in the adjoining Refectory)
- The Bramante Cloister
- Chapel of St. Corona with frescoes by Guadenzio Ferrari
- *Crowning of Thorns*, Titian
- Madonna delle Grazie Chapel
- *Madonna delle Grazie delivering Milan from the Plague*, Il Cerano

INFORMATION

- ✚ B2
- ✉ Piazza Santa Maria delle Grazie, 20123
- ☎ 02 4801 4248
- 🕐 Mon–Sat 7–12, 3–7; Sun, public hols 7.15–12.15, 3.30–7 (no visits during services)
- 🚇 Conciliazione
- 🚌 18; tram 16
- ♿ Good; three steps
- 🎫 Free; English guide to church and *Last Supper* expensive
- ↔ Corso Magenta (▶ 27)
- ❓ You need to book at least two days in advance to view the *Last Supper*, Reservations ☎ 02 8942 1146

While *The Last Supper* is a real highlight, the church itself should not be missed. Although it was built over a mere 26 years, it gives the impression of two completely different churches.

Renaissance gem Guiniforte Solari designed the church for the Dominican Order in 1463–90. The contrast of styles between the Dominican late-Gothic nave, with its wealth of decoration, and the pure, harmonious domed apse built by Bramante marks the rapid change that came with the Renaissance. In 1943, a bomb destroyed the cloister, but miraculously, two of its greatest treasures, the *Last Supper* and the Dome, survived.

Glorious architecture The magnificent brick and terracotta exterior, crowned by Bramante's grand dome, is best seen from Corso Magenta. From the Renaissance portal, you enter Solari's nave, with its richly decorated arches and vaults. Beyond it, Bramante's apse feels simple in comparison, the decoration limited to graffiti and remnants of frescoes. The beautiful Bramante Cloister, surrounding a garden, is familiarly known as Chiostrino delle Rane after the bronze frogs (*rane*) at the fountain. If a service is in progress, you can reach the cloister via the street entrance on Via Caradosso.

Leonardo's masterpiece Ludovico Il Moro commissioned this fresco in the refectory adjoining the church in 1494, and it is one of the most famous in the world. Unfortunately the experimental techniques used by Leonardo led to signs of deterioration within 20 years of completing the work. Much restoration has been done, the latest in 1999, in an attempt to return the painting to its former glory. Booking in advance is compulsory.

Parco Sempione

A welcome break from the traffic of the city with a fine view of the Castello Sforzesco, the Parco Sempione was originally part of the vast hunting ground of the Sforza family, who occupied the castle. It became a public park in the late 19th century.

Early uses In the early 1800s the French used the land as an exercise ground for their armed forces. Napoleon had plans to build a great piazza around the castle and turn the whole area into the new heart of the city, but apart from the Arco della Pace and the Arena (▶ 60) the plans never materialized. The public park, 47ha (116 acres) in size, was begun in 1893 when Emilio Alemagna landscaped the area on the lines of an English park—as was the fashion.

The country in town The gardens stretch from the castle to the Arco della Pace—a landscape of lawns, large trees, winding paths and a lake with a small bridge. On the west side, you can't miss the Torre Branca, an Eiffel Tower-like steel structure (1933) that's now open night and day after many years of closure. The Florentine designer Roberto Cavalli has opened a restaurant at the base of the tower (▶ 64). The nearby Palazzo dell'Arte, a rather austere building, was opened a year before the tower as a permanent site of the Triennale Decorative Arts Exhibition. The park is dotted with modern sculpture and monuments, and has lots for children, with a play area, mini-train rides and sailing boats on the lake. The paths are popular with cyclists, joggers, dog-walkers and Sunday strollers and there's entertainment in the summer months. Although the park is open late into the evening, it is best avoided after dark.

HIGHLIGHTS

- Arena Civica
- Torre Branca
- *Bagni Misteriosi*, sculpture by Giorgio de Chirico found behind the Palazzo dell'Arte
- View of Arco della Pace from the lake

INFORMATION

- ✠ B1
- ✉ Piazza Castello–Piazza Sempione (eight entrances around perimeter)
- ☎ Torre Branca: 02 331 4120
- 🕐 Park: daily 6.30am–8/9/10/11.30pm depending on season. Torre Branca: Tue, Thu 9.30pm–1am; Wed 10.30–12.30, 4–6.30, 8.30–1; Sat, Sun 10.30–2,2.30–7, 8.30–1. Winter hours are shorter; check before visiting. Closed in bad weather
- 🍴 Cafés in park
- Ⓜ Cadorna, Cairioli, Lanza, Moscova
- 🚌 43, 57, 61, 94; tram 1, 4, 27
- 🎟 Park free; Torre Branca moderate, over 60s and children under 3 free
- ↔ Arco della Pace (▶ 30), Castello Sforzesco and Museo d'Arte Antica (▶ 34)

Arco della Pace

HIGHLIGHTS

- The huge bronze Chariot of Peace (25m/82ft high)
- A distant view from the Parco Sempione
- The initial impact as you approach from Corso Sempione

INFORMATION

- B1
- Piazza Sempione, 20154 and 20145
- Café
- 57, 61; tram 1, 30
- Good
- Parco Sempione (➤ 29)

A detail of the Chariot of Peace, on top of the Arco della Pace

Milan's triumphal arch was intended as a monument to Napoleon's victories. With his fall from power in 1814, the project came to a standstill and he was never to see its completion.

Napoleon's dream The Arch of Victories, as it was at first known, was finally finished in 1838 under the Austrian Emperor, Ferdinand I. In commemoration of the European Peace Treaty of 1815 he changed the name to the Arch of Peace (Arco della Pace) and made appropriate changes to the bas-reliefs. The formal monument marks the northwest end of the Parco Sempione, and the start of the Corso Sempione, Napoleon's highway to the Simplon Pass.

Monumental construction The arch was designed by Luigi Cagnola and inspired by the arch of Septimius Severus in the Forum in Rome. Work began in 1807, halted in 1814, and resumed in 1826 under Ferdinand I of Austria. The circular piazza around it was redesigned in the 1980s and closed to traffic. The arch is best seen from a distance, preferably from the park side where you can see the Chariot of Peace on the top of the monument. The large reclining figures on the upper level represent four rivers in French-occupied northern Italy: the Po, Ticino, Adda and Tagliamento. A recent facelift has returned the arch to its former glory and the marble gleams once again.

Beyond the arch The two buildings either side of the arch on the park side were toll houses. The Corso Sempione on the far side was based on the grand boulevards of Paris, although it's not nearly as chic. Open-air concerts are held in the circular piazza on summer evenings, but otherwise the area is best avoided after dark.

Basilica di Sant'Ambrogio

Named for the city's patron saint, Sant'Ambrogio is a supreme example of Romanesque architecture and a prototype for many 11th- and 12th-century Lombard churches.

Years in the building The church, west of the Duomo, was originally built between AD379 and 386 by Bishop Ambrogio, who was later made patron saint of Milan. It was dedicated to saints Gervasius and Protasius whose remains had been discovered on the site, but was renamed following Ambrogio's death. The church was enlarged in the ninth and eleventh centuries, although Bramante's Portico della Canonica was left unfinished until the 17th century, and had to be reconstructed after the 1943 bombings.

Superb decoration This is one of the loveliest churches in the city, occupying a large complex with lots to see. The fine red brick exterior, with its two bell towers (ninth-century one to the right, 12th-century one to the left) is best seen from Piazza Sant'Ambrogio. Access to the church is via the lovely Ansperto atrium, which was built as a refuge for pilgrims. The church interior, simple and harmonious, has three aisles and distinctive ribbed cross vaulting. The apse is embellished with mosaics (sixth- to eighth-century, much restored) depicting Christ between Milanese saints and martyrs.

Not to be missed Beautifully carved in the 4th century, the Sarcophagus of Stilicho, below the pulpit and left of the nave, is traditionally believed to be the tomb of the Roman Military Commander Stilicho and his wife and is one of the few surviving features of the original church. The pulpit above it was constructed from 12th-century fragments.

HIGHLIGHTS

- Sacrophagus of Stilicho
- 10th-century *ciborium* (canopy)
- Ninth-century altar front sculpted by Volvinio and encrusted with gems, gold and silver
- Chapel of San Vittore in Ciel d'Oro with fifth-century dome mosaic.
- Underground crypt with remains of saints Ambrogio, Gervasius and Portasius in a single urn

INFORMATION

- ✚ C3
- ✉ Piazza Sant'Ambrogio 15, 20123
- ☎ 02 8645 0895
- 🕐 Mon–Sat 7–12, 2.30–7; Sun, hols 7–1, 3–8. No visits during services
- 🚇 Sant'Ambrogio
- 🚌 50, 58, 94
- ♿ Good; entrance on Via Lanzone 30
- 🎟 Free; Chapel of San Vittore in Ciel d'Oro inexpensive
- 🔗 Museo Nazionale della Scienza e della Tecnica (► 26)

Top **25**

7

Civico Museo Archeologico

Milan was once a powerful Roman city and this museum, in the ruins of the Benedictine Maggiore monastery, exhibits some fine examples of Roman sculpture and everyday items.

Moving collections The exhibits were formerly housed in the Castello Sforzesco in the city's archaeological and numismatic collections. Following World War II, several sections were transferred here, next to the church of San Maurizio, with some remaining in the Castello. The monastery, once the largest women's convent in Milan was built in the ninth century, rebuilt in the early 16th, and was badly bombed in 1943.

Roman and other finds Fragments of Roman funerary stones, sarcophagi and capitals are arranged around the cloister at the front of the museum, with pride of place going to the Masso di Bormo, a large stone whose carvings date back to the third millennium BC. Inside, a model of Roman Milan (Mediolanum) introduces the Roman collection. The basement is devoted to Greek and Etruscan exhibits and a tiny section to works of art from Gandha-ra (what is now northern Pakistan and Afghanistan). If time is short concentrate on the Roman exhibits and leave out the lower ground floor. Take a look at the Coppa Trivulzio in the Roman section, which is behind the black screen and quite easy to miss. It is an exquisite late fourth-century goblet in emerald green glass, carved from a single piece of glass. Take heart in the inscription below the rim: '*Bibe vivas multi annis*' ('drink and you will live for many years'). The Parabiago Plate in the Roman section, on the left is a large silver-gilt, embossed *patera* (weighing 3.5kg/8lb) discovered in 1907, from Parabiago, northwest of Milan.

HIGHLIGHTS

- Coppa Trivulzio
- Parabiago Plate
- The torso of Hercules. It was discovered among ruins of Roman baths on what is now Corso Europa.
- *Portrait of Maximin* (mid 3rd-century AD); one of a series of portraits dating from Caesar's era.

INFORMATION

- ✚ C2
- ✉ Corso Magenta 15, 20123
- ☎ 02 8645 0011
- 🕐 Tue–Sun 9–5.30
- Ⓠ Cadorna, Cairoli
- 🚌 50, 58; tram 18, 19
- ♿ Poor; phone ahead
- 🎫 Free
- ↔ Corso Magenta (➤ 27), Baslica di Sant'Ambrogio (➤ 31), San Maurizio (➤ 33)
- ℹ Small booklets in English, inexpensive

Stone carving

32

San Maurizio

The unremarkable grey baroque façade of this church on the busy Corso Magenta gives no hint of the glorious interior. Step inside and you are greeted by a riot of beautiful baroque frescoes, decorating every surface.

Important convent The church was built in 1503 for the adjoining Monastero Maggiore, formerly one of the most prestigious monasteries in Milan, and home to Benedictine nuns. The monastery was largely destroyed in the 19th century but is today the site of the Museo Archeologico. A schedule of restoration of the church frescoes has been ongoing since 1986.

Church meets state The church was constructed in two main parts: one hall for the congregation and a larger cloistered hall for the nuns. The two were separated by a partition wall and altar, which face you as you go into the church. The nuns were able to participate in Eucharist celebrated in the public hall through the little doors, which you can see in the arch in the central fresco to the left of the altar; they could also receive Communion through the tiny opening (the *comunichino*) on the right of the altar below the figure of Christ.

Wonderful frescoes On both sides of the partition wall, the main subject of the decoration is the Passion of Christ. Many of the frescoes were executed by Bernardino Luini (c.1480–1532), one of the most prominent Lombard followers of Leonardo da Vinci; the chapels on the left were decorated by his pupils. Unlike most churches in Milan, the lighting here is good and you can actually see the frescoes in detail. The nun's hall makes a splendid setting for the series of classical concerts that are held here in winter.

HIGHLIGHTS

- Frescoes by Bernardino Luini including *Life of St. Catherine*
- *The Adoration of the Magi*, Antonio Campi
- Frescoes by unattributed artists

INFORMATION

- C2
- Corso Magenta 15, 20123
- Tue–Sun 9–12, 2–5.30 (can sometimes close for no reason); closed 1 Jan, 1 May, Christmas
- Cadorna
- 50, 58; tram 18, 19
- Poor
- Free
- Corso Magenta (► 27), Basilica di Sant'Ambrogio (► 31), Museo Archeologico (► 32)
- Guidebooks in Italian only

Castello Sforzesco e Museo d'Arte Antica

- Mausoleum of Bernabò Visconti (1363), Bonino da Campione
- Salle delle Asse with fresco decoration attributed to Leonardo
- Sala degli Scarlioni: Michaelangelo's *Rondanini Pietà* (1554–64) and Gaston de Foix' funerary monument, Agostini Busti

INFORMATION

- 🔒 C2
- ✉ Piazza Castello, 20121
- ☎ 02 8846 3700/3
- 🕐 Castello: daily 9–5.30. Museums: Tue–Sun 9–5.30. Castle and museum closed 1 Jan, Easter, 1 May, 25 Dec
- Ⓖ Cadorna, Cairoli
- 🚌 57; tram 1, 4, 27
- ♿ Good; some steps
- 💵 Free
- ↔ Parco Sempione (▶ 29)
- 🛈 Guidebooks available

A landmark of Milan, the castle is a vast brick quadrilateral, dominated on the town side by the Filarete Tower. It stands as a symbol of the Golden Renaissance Age, and today is home to the excellent civic museums.

Through the centuries Built as a fortress by the Visconti family between 1358 and 1368, the castle was all but demolished after their downfall. It was transformed into a Renaissance fort under Francesco Sforza, and his son, who became Duke of Milan, turned it into a sumptuous residence. By the early 19th century, Napoleon turned what was left of the building into soldiers' quarters. In 1884, the city planned a virtual demolition of the castle, but the architect Luca Beltrami transformed it into a museum.

Exploring the museums Start your visit at the entrance under the Filarete Tower. Beyond the massive Piazza d'Armi is the Renaissance Corte Ducale, residence of the Sforzas, around which the Civiche Raccolte d'Arte Antica is displayed. This rich collection of sculpture spans 12 centuries, from a fourth-century sarcophagus to Michelangelo's *Rondanini*—the highlight of the whole collection. On the upper floor is the furniture collection and the Art Gallery, whose Italian Renaissance masterpieces include works by Mantegna, Giovanni Bellini, Antonella da Messina and Filippo Lippi as well as a rich collection of works by Lombard artists. The third courtyard, La Rochetta, has charming porticoes that were originally embellished by frescoes. The first and second floors are devoted to the applied arts, which include an outstanding collection of musical instruments and the rare Trivulzio Tapestries, designed by Bramantino. The basement houses the Archaeology Museum.

San Lorenzo Maggiore

This huge fourth-century basilica may have been the chapel of the imperial Roman palace. The greatest treasure is the Sant'Aquilino Chapel, once entirely covered in frescoes and mosaics.

Founded on a Roman temple The church can be found in the Ticinese quarter, outside the Roman walls, southwest of the city. It is also known as San Lorenzo alle Colonne, named after the colonnade outside the church dating from the second and third centuries. The 16 columns and the section of architrave were probably part of a temple and were placed here in the fourth century when construction began on the basilica. Built with marble from Roman buildings nearby, the basilica was founded on what was thought to be a Roman amphitheatre. It was subsequently rebuilt in the 12th century, with further rebuilding between 1573 and 1619 by Martino Bassi.

Beautiful chapel You can't miss the church—it has the largest dome in Milan and an unconvincing monument to Constantine in front, which is a bronze copy of a Roman statue. The interior, octagonal in form and crowned by the dome, is striking for its sheer size. Inside, make for the Capella di Sant'Aquilino, which may have been added as a mausoleum; its small chapel houses the saint's remains in a silver urn. The 12th-century fresco of *The Deposition* can be seen at the entrance to the chapel, on the left hand side. Here you will find the remarkable fourth- or fifth-century mosaics of Christ and the Apostles, and Elijah on the Chariot of Fire. Steps behind the altar take you down to the foundations of the church.

HIGHLIGHTS

- Capella di Sant'Aquilino
- Fourth/fifth-century mosaics
- 12th-century fresco
- The view of the church from Parco delle Basiliche, the garden behind the church

INFORMATION

- ✚ C3
- ✉ Corso di Porta Ticinese 39, 20123
- ☎ 02 8940 4129
- 🕐 Daily 7.30–6.45; Capella di Sant'Aquilino daily 9.30–6.30
- Ⓜ Missori
- 🚌 94; tram 3
- ♿ Good
- 💰 Free; Capella di Sant'Aquilino inexpensive

This statue of Emperor Constantine stands outside San Lorenzo Maggiore

Basilica di Sant'Eustorigo

INFORMATION

➕ C3

✉ Piazza Sant'Eustorgio 1,
20122

☎ 02 8940 2671

🕐 Church: daily 7–12,
3.30–6 ; Museum:
Tue–Sun 10–6

🚊 Tram 3, 9, 30

♿ Good (ramp to church)

🎫 Church: free; museum:
moderate

The unassuming neo-Romanesque façade of the Basilica of Sant'Eustorgio belies the wonderful earlier interior architecture and superb frescoes, which make this one of the most interesting churches to visit in the city.

Early beginnings The much-restored basilica was built on a Christian cemetery on the road to Pavia. The original church was founded by St. Eustorgius in the fourth century but was completely destroyed by Frederick Barbarossa in 1162. Reconstruction began in 1190 and lasted for several centuries. This included the building of the bell tower in 1306, the first in Milan to be fitted with a clock. The final alteration came in 1865 with the building of the façade seen today.

Exquisite chapel The single aisle church conveys a sense of huge space, and this includes the gem of Renaissance Lombard architecture, the Capella Portinari (c.1462), which is accessed via the museum beside the church. It was the work of the Tuscan, Michelozzo, and is often likened to Brunelleschi's Pazzi Chapel in Florence. The chapel was built to house the remains of St. Peter Martyr and is embellished with Vincenzo Foppa's glorious frescoes of 1468. In the middle of the chapel is the tomb of St. Peter—moved here in 1734—with the magnificent marble Arca di San Pietro Martire carved by Giovanni di Balduccio in 1339. His work marks a milestone in Lombard sculpture's move towards the Renaissance, a harmonious blending of the classical Renaissance and sinuous vibrant Gothic line.

Museum in the cloisters The monastery adjoining the church is the property of the Diocesan museum and has 17th- and 18th-century religious relics and works of art from the Basilica.

Pinacoteca Ambrosiana

Cardinal Federico Borromeo built the Palazzo Ambrosiana in 1608 to house his collection of books and manuscripts. The art collection includes outstanding works by 15th- and 16th-century Italian and Flemish masters.

Phenomenal collection In the early 17th century, Cardinal Federico Borromeo commissioned eight experts to travel through Europe and the Middle East to amass a collection for his library. The Biblioteca Ambrosiana was set up with around 30,000 prints and 14,000 manuscripts. Nine years later, his personal collection of 127 paintings was added to form the Pinacoteca Ambrosiana. The building was extended in the 19th century, and today is run by a private and autonomous ecclesiastical foundation. From 1990 to 1997 the gallery closed for radical restructure; 10 new rooms were made accessible, enabling around 400 paintings to be displayed. Works by Leonardo, Titian, Raphael and Caravaggio are among those exhibited.

Essential viewing for any art lover The ground floor library contains the *Codex Atlanticus*, with over 1,000 pages of drawings by Leonardo da Vinci—only accessible to scholars. On the first floor, the gallery consists of 24 rooms: Rooms 1 and 4–7 display the Borromeo collection: Tuscan, Lombard and Venetian Renaissance and 17th-century Flemish art. The drawings displayed under glass are Leonardo reproductions. Rooms 2 and 3 display Renaissance masterpieces added later to the collection. Rooms 8–24 have 16th- to 20th-century paintings, sculpture and *objets d'art*, culminating in Manfredo Settala's diverse collection of scientific instruments, gemstones, exotic animals, books and paintings.

HIGHLIGHTS

- Room 1: *Adoration of the Magi*, Titian
- Room 2: *The Musician*, Leonardo da Vinci
- Room 5: Raphael's cartoon for the *School of Athens* (1510), representing the greatest philosophers and mathematicians in conference
- Room 5: Caravaggio's staggeringly realistic *Basket of Fruit* (1594)

INFORMATION

www.ambrosiana.it

- C3
- Piazza Pio XI, 20123
- 02 806 921
- Tue–Sun 10–5:30 (ticket office closes 4:30)
- Cordusio
- Tram 2, 3, 14, 19, 24
- Good
- Expensive
- Santa Maria presso San Satiro (➤ 38), Piazza Mercanti (➤ 39)
- Guidebooks and catalogues; shop sells good art books

Santa Maria presso San Satiro

HIGHLIGHTS

- Octagonal Renaissance baptistery with terracottas by De Fondutis
- Bell tower
- *Virgin of the Miracle*, 13th-century fresco over the high altar
- Capella della Pietà

INFORMATION

- ✛ D3
- ✉ Via Torino 9, 20123
- ☎ 02 7202 1804
- ⏰ Mon–Fri 7.30–11.30, 3.30–6.30; Sat, Sun, public hols 9–12, 3.15–7 (no visits during services)
- Ⓜ Duomo
- 🚊 Tram 2, 3, 14, 15, 16, 24
- ♿ Poor
- 🎫 Free
- ↔ Palazzo Reale e Museo del Duomo (► 42), Duomo (► 43)

This gem of a church is squeezed between four streets southwest of the Duomo. The original ninth-century building was brilliantly restructured by Donato Bramante, who created the illusion of depth by using gilded stucco and *trompe l'oeil*.

Miraculous design The original church was built in the ninth century and dedicated to St. Satiro (St. Ambrogio's brother), St. Ambrogio and St. Silvestro. In 1478, Bramante was commissioned to remodel the church—he was the architect who was later to restructure the church of Santa Maria delle Grazie (► 28) and in 1506 was to produce the first designs for the new St. Peter's Basilica in Rome. The new church had to provide a safe haven for an image of the Madonna with Child thought to have miraculous powers. Legend goes that when the fresco was attacked in 1242, the Virgin bled; she was placed above the high altar and remains there today.

Small but beautiful Bramante designed the church on the lines of a Roman basilica with a Greek Cross plan, but retained the Romanesque bell tower (the oldest in Lombardy) and the apse known as the Sacellum of San Satiro or Capella della Pietà—although this has since been reworked. The chapel is reached from the left transept and had early medieval frescoes and a terracotta Pietà scene (1482–83) by De Fondutis. The façade was not completed until the second half of the 19th century in neo-Renaissance style. The presbytery is only about a metre (3ft) deep, but Bramante's ingenious use of *trompe l'oeil* gives the impression of a genuine apse. It is worth having a look from Via Falcone to view the rear façade.

The font in the baptistery

Piazza Mercanti

For centuries the administrative and commercial hub of the city, this central market square is rich in architecture and history. Rather more intimate than most piazzas in Milan, it is traffic-free and preserves its medieval character.

Origins The first buildings in this piazza were established in the 13th century and the square was enclosed by six gates, accessible only to the citizens of the quarter. The Palazzo della Ragione, built between 1228 and 1233 (➤ 57), served as the city's law courts for over five centuries, and its loggia was used for medieval market stalls. Notaries used to draft their documents from portable desks around the palazzo and banns were declared from the Loggia degli Orsi.

Intimate appeal The piazza used to be much bigger, stretching to the far side of the present-day Via Mercanti, the wide pedestrian thoroughfare. On the north side is the huge Palazzo dei Giureconsulti, which houses the Chamber of Commerce. The Loggia degli Orsi, facing the Palazzo della Ragione, is a lovely pink-and-grey marble building that immediately draws the eye. The ground floor arcade, now a bank, was used as a market. The coats of arms above are those of patrician families who lived in the quarter. Today, the piazza is a popular rendezvous, a pleasant spot for browsing in *bouquinistes*, lunching alfresco, or just sitting on the steps of the Palazzo della Ragione, soaking up the architecture. The central well with two Ionic columns supporting a pediment dates from the 16th century. Unlike the nearby Piazza del Duomo, which is large and impersonal, the Piazza Mercanti has retained its intimate and historic charm and even McDonald's at the east end manages to keep a low profile.

HIGHLIGHTS

- Loggia degli Orsi
- Palazzo delle Scuole Palatine (1645), a baroque palace with sculptures of St. Augustine and the Latin poet, Ausonius
- Palazzo Panigarola, a handsome building with Gothic ogee arches

INFORMATION

- ➕ D2
- ✉ Piazza Mercanti, 20123
- 🚇 Duomo
- 🚋 Tram 2, 3, 14, 15, 24
- 🍴 Ristorante al Mercante (café with outdoor tables, ➤ 65)
- ↔ Duomo (➤ 43)

Teatro alla Scala

DID YOU KNOW?

- The opera house has exceptionally fine acoustics
- The stage is one of the largest in the world measuring 1,200sq m (4,300sq ft)
- Most of the world's best-known conductors and opera singers have performed here
- Tickets are notoriously hard to get, so book well in advance (performances sell out months in advance)

INFORMATION

www.teatroallascala.org
- D2
- Piazza della Scala, 20121
- La Scala Information Point and La Scala Bookstore (Piazza della Scala 5) 02 869 2260
- Opera season opening night always 7 Dec, feast day of Sant'Ambrogio, patron saint of Milan
- Duomo, Cordusio
- 61; tram 1, 2
- Price depends on performance; museum moderate
- Good
- Galleria Vittorio Emanuele II (➤ 44)

The world famous La Scala, built by Empress Maria Theresa of Austria, has seen the premières of many great classical Italian operas. The façade on Piazza della Scala is surprisingly sober, and belies the sumptuous auditorium.

Major overhaul The opera house, closed in 2002 for a major revamp, reopened for the 2004/2005 opera season. After two years, Italian opera has returned to its true home.

World famous The opera house takes its name from the Santa Maria della Scala, the church on whose site it was built in 1776–78. It was built by Giuseppe Piermarini, architect of the Palazzo Reale and took the place of the smaller Regio Ducale Teatro, which had been destroyed by fire. After the 1943 bombings, La Scala was the first of the city's monuments to be rebuilt. It reopened in 1946 and was re-inaugurated by Toscanini. The former artistic director came back from America after 17 years, having fled from Fascist Italy in 1929. After his death in New York in 1957, his coffin was flown to Milan and laid in the foyer of La Scala where thousands lined up to pay their last respects. Musical works by Rossini, Donizetti, Bellini, Verdi and Puccini had their debuts here, not always to great acclaim—the first night of Puccini's Madame Butterfly in 1904 was a complete fiasco—no one liked it!

Sumptious interior The plush auditorium is decorated in red velvet and gilded stuccowork, with a 365-lamp crystal chandelier; it has an overall seating capacity of 2,015. You can view the auditorium as part of a museum tour. The Museo Teatrale alla Scala (➤ 53) contains a huge collection of theatrical memorabilia among its interesting exhibits.

Pinacoteca di Brera

The Brera gallery gives you the chance to see one of the very finest collections of northern Italian paintings. From small beginnings, it was enlarged by Napoleon to include works by the region's major artists.

Impressive collection The gallery is in the Palazzo Brera, a baroque palace built on the site of a 14th-century Jesuit convent. Empress Maria Theresa of Austria evicted the Jesuits, redesigned the palace in neoclassical style and founded the Accademia di Belle Arti in 1773. The Pinacoteca opened in 1809, showing mostly works that had been confiscated by Napoleon from churches and convents in French-occupied territories: Lombardy, Veneto, Emilia-Romagna and the Marche. Through donations and exchanges, the collection has been growing every since. In 1882, the Accademia di Belle Arti and the Pinacoteca became independent, and the gallery became a state-owned art museum.

An art lover's heaven The works of art are arranged in 30 large rooms, making for pleasant viewing. Although the collection spans six centuries and includes some non-Italian artists (El Greco, Anthony Van Dyck, Peter Paul Rubens, Rembrandt), the emphasis is on northern Italian 15th–16th century art. The collection is full of gems by the leading Renaissance masters, with the Venetian collection the largest and most important outside Venice. Here, too, you have a chance to study the Lombard masters of the Renaissance. The two most famous paintings in the collection are the *Montefeltro Altarpiece* (1472–74) by Piero della Francesca, which demonstrates the artist's fascination with geometry, and Raphael's *Marriage of the Virgin* (1504), the greatest work of his Perugian period.

HIGHLIGHTS

● Jesi Collection – paintings and sculpture from the first half of the 19th century
● *Dead Christ*, Mantegna
● Portraits by Lotto, Tintoretto, Titian
● *Supper at Emmaus* (1606), Caravaggio
● *Virgin of the Rose Garden*, Bernardino Luini
● *The Kiss* (1859), Francesco Hayez

INFORMATION

www.brera.beniculturali.it
✚ D2
✉ Via Brera 28, 20121
☎ 02 722 631
🕐 Tue–Sun 8.30–7.15 (last admission 45 minutes before closing). Closed 1 Jan, 1 May, 25 Dec
🚇 Lanza, Montenapoleone
🚋 61, tram 1, 27
♿ Good, lift
💶 Moderate
ℹ Audiotours, good book and souvenir shop

41

Palazzo Reale e Museo del Duomo

HIGHLIGHTS

All in Museo del Duomo:
- Plans for the Duomo
- Huge, elaborate wooden model of the Duomo
- A stainless steel copy of the original iron support that lifted the Maddonina to the top of the Duomo in 1774

INFORMATION

- ✚ D3
- ✉ Palazzo Reale: Piazza del Duomo 12; Museo del Duomo: Piazza del Duomo 14, 20122
- ☎ Museo del Duomo 02 860 358
- ◷ Palazzo Reale: depends on exhibitions. Closed Mon. Museo del Duomo: Daily 10–1.15, 3–6. Both closed 1 Jan, Easter, 25 April, 1 May, 15 Aug, Christmas
- Ⓜ Duomo
- 🚊 Tram 2, 3, 14, 15, 19, 24 and others
- ♿ Palazzo Reale Good. Museo del Duomo Moderate
- 💶 Palazzo Reale: Museo della Reggia free. Temporary exhibition prices vary. Museo del Duomo: expensive
- ↔ Duomo (► 43), Galleria Vittorio Emanuele II (► 44)
- 🛈 Palazzo Reale bookshop for temporary exhibitions only; books and cards at Museo del Duomo

In the heart of the city, beside (and inevitably dwarfed by) the Duomo, this historic palace was seat of the city council in the 11th century, ducal residence of the Viscontis and Sforzas, and the royal palace of the Austrian rulers.

A plethora of museums The Palazzo has been rebuilt several times, the present-day building owing its neoclassical appearance to the 1770s redevelopment of the square. The interior is a mere shadow of its former self and there is much on-going restoration. But it's worth a visit for the Museo del Duomo, the Museo della Reggia, the pre-1990 works from the Civico Museo d'Arte Contemporanea (CIMAC) Contemporary Art collection, and for the major contemporary art exhibitions that are held here.

History of art The 11th-century Palazzo Broletto Vecchio (Courthouse) was rebuilt by the ruling Viscontis between 1330 and 1336, and subsequently redesigned in the 16th century by the Sforzas. Mozart performed at the theatre here in 1770, when he was 14. In the following decade the palace was rebuilt by Giuseppe Piermarini. Large sections of the palace were demolished in the 1920s and 30s, and most of its dazzling interior was destroyed in the bombings of 1943. In the 1960s, the city bought the palace for use as museums, offices and to display art exhibitions. CIMAC was housed here in 1983 and has a fine collection of paintings including works by Pablo Picasso and Henri Matisse. The first-floor Museo della Reggia, has Gobelin tapestries and frescoes. The Museo del Duomo (in a wing of the palace to the left of the main entrance) houses a rich collection of paintings, sculptures, stained glass windows and a vast array of religious objects from the Duomo.

Duomo

Symbol of the city, the sumptuous Duomo, with its huge proportions, towers over the Piazza Duomo below. An ascent to the roof reveals a wonderful panorama of Milan and beyond.

Dazzling and ethereal The Duomo bristles with Gothic statues, gargoyles, pinnacles and soaring spires and has attracted comments from the censorious 'an imitation hedgehog' (D.H. Lawrence) to the lyrical 'a poem of marble' (Mark Twain). Ascend to the roof, by steps or lift (elevator), for a wonderful panorama of Milan and, on a clear day, a view as far as the Alps.

Controversial building Milan's Duomo was founded in 1386 under the ambitious Gian Galeazzo Visconti, who resolved to build the biggest church in Italy. Although the church was consecrated in 1418, it remained incomplete for over four centuries. Work finally started on the façade in the early 17th century, but it gave rise to decades of controversy and was only finished in 1812, under Napoleon.

Into the darkness The Duomo is 157m (515ft) long, 33m (108ft) wide across the nave and 92m (302ft) across the transept; the roof is decorated with 2,245 statues, 135 spires and 96 gargoyles; the interior can hold 40,000 people. It is topped by the Madonnina, (the little Madonna), a gilded copper statue hoisted up here in 1774. After the stunning white exterior, the interior feels gloomy, the darkness emphasized by heavy funeral monuments and the 52 hefty piers defining the five aisles. In the darkness, your eye is drawn to the lively stained glass windows. Tombs and monuments in the church include the extraordinary statue of *The Flayed San Bartolomeo* (1562) with his skin draped over his shoulders.

HIGHLIGHTS

- The roof and the view
- The apse
- Stained glass windows
- Trivulzio Candelabra (12th-century crafted in gold)
- Treasury's collection of gold and silverwork
- The elaborate Crypt

INFORMATION

- D2
- Piazza del Duomo, 20121
- 02 8646 3456
- Opening times: Cathedral daily 7–7 ; Treasury and crypt: daily 9–12, 2.30–6, Baptistery: daily 9.45–12.45, 2–5.45; Roof: Mar–end Oct daily 9–5.30; Nov–end Feb 9–4.15
- Duomo
- Tram 1, 2, 3, 15, 24 and others
- Main cathedral good. Crypt and Treasury not accessible
- Cathedral free, Roof entrance steps and lift moderate. Combined Museo del Duomo and Treasury moderate, combined Museo, Roof and Treasury expensive
- Palazzo Reale e Museo del Duomo (▶ 42), Galleria Vittorio Emanuele II (▶ 44)
- Palazzo Reale bookshop for temporary exhibitions only; books and cards at Museo del Duomo

43

(see below)

Galleria Vittorio Emanuele II

HIGHLIGHTS

- Watching the fashionable Milanese
- Savini's restaurant
- Zucca–have a cocktail or a coffee in the famous period café (➤ 71)
- Excellent boutique shopping

INFORMATION

➕ D2

✉ Galleria Vittorio Emanuele II, 20121

🍴 Plenty (see highlights above)

Ⓜ Duomo

🚌 61; tram 1, 2, 3, 14, 15, 24

♿ Good

🔄 Duomo (➤ 43)

High-budget shopping in Galleria Vittorio Emanuele II

Linking Piazza del Duomo and Piazza della Scala, this elegant glass-roofed arcade has long been a popular rendezvous for the Milanese. It's worth indulging in a pricey cappuccino to watch the perpetual *passeggiata* of fashionable locals.

City reconstruction It was in 1865, after Unification, that the architect Giuseppe Mengoni offered his silver trowel to King Vittorio Emanuele II—after whom the arcade was named—to lay the foundation stone of the Galleria. Sadly, Mengoni fell to his death from the scaffolding a few days before the inauguration in 1897. The project's completion, in 1898, was marked by building a triumphal arch at the Duomo end. The creation of the arcade and the colossal demolition process that it involved reshaped the whole structure of the city.

Glitzy Milan This is a great place for shopping, eating and drinking—if you can afford it. The glass roof gives the arcade a feeling of light and space, even on a dull day. There are excellent bookshops, music stores, and leather and clothes boutiques. A focal point is the central octagon area, under the glass dome, 47m (154ft) high. Pavement mosaics depict the coats of arms of the Savoy family and the symbols of Italian cities: Milan (red cross on a white background), Turin (a bull), Florence (a lily) and Rome (a she-wolf). Milanese tradition has it that stepping on the genitalia of the bull will bring you good luck. Savini's (➤ 64), one of Milan's finest restaurants, is traditionally the meeting place of opera fans after first nights at La Scala.

Museo Poldi Pezzoli

The palace and its exquisite collection of paintings and decorative arts belonged to Gian Giacomo Poldi Pezzoli, a 19th-century Milanese aristocrat. Each room was planned to evoke a style of the past.

Stunning collection With the considerable fortune that he inherited from both sides of the family, Poldi Pezzoli (1822–79) amassed a large collection of antiques and art, the nucleus of which was his remarkable armoury. With the advice of leading experts, Poldi Pezzoli built up a collection of armour, furniture, textiles, ceramics, bronzes and *objets d'art*. Pride of place, however, goes to his fabulous collection of paintings. On his death, he left the palace and its contents 'to the use and benefit of the public'. The building was badly bombed in 1943, but was rebuilt, retaining the original decoration where possible. Through gifts and bequests, the museum considerably enlarged its collection in the 1970s and 80s.

Art and armour The two floors of exhibits are connected by a charming staircase with landscape paintings and a black marble fountain. The ground floor rooms are devoted to the Armoury, in its stunning new neo-Gothic setting, the Fresco Room, the textile collections and library. The main collections are upstairs: paintings from the 14th–16th-century Lombard School, northern Italian works of art from the 14th–18th centuries, and the Salone Dorato or Golden Room, which is full of Renaissance masterpieces. Visits take you through the Black Room, so called because the walls were once covered in ebony, the lavish little neo-Gothic Dante study and a series of rooms with showcases of jewellery, sundials and antique clocks and watches.

HIGHLIGHTS

In the Salone Dorato:
- *Portrait of a Young Woman*, Piero del Pollaiuolo–this lovely portrait has become a symbol of the palace.
- *Pietà and Madonna and Child*, Sandro Botticelli
- *St. Nicholas of Tolentino*, Piero della Francesca
- *Madonna* and *Child*, Andrea Mantegna
- *Pietà*, Giovanni Bellini

INFORMATION

- D2
- Via Manzoni 12, 20121
- 02 79 48 89
- Tue–Sun 10–6; closed 1 Jan, Easter, 25 Apr, 1 May, 1 & 15 Aug, 1 Nov, 8, 25 & 26 Dec
- Montenapoleone
- 61, 94; tram 1, 2,
- Poor but ground floor possible
- Expensive
- Teatro alla Scala (► 40), Quadrilatero d'Oro (► 46)
- Audiotours, shop

Quadrilatero d'Oro

HIGHLIGHTS

- Cova at Via Montenapoleone 8 (► 70), a historic café with tantalizing window displays of patisserie, sweets and chocolates. Sip coffee at the bar or sit in one of the smart salons with well-dressed Milanese.
- One of the best spots in Europe to window shop
- Aristocratic residences

INFORMATION

- ✚ E2
- ✉ 20121
- 🕐 Varied. Most shops close on Sundays and Mondays, though some are open on Monday afternoon. Most open at 9am or 10.30am
- 🍴 Numerous with some very chic ones
- Ⓜ San Babila, Montenapoleone
- 🚌 61, 94; tram 1, 2,
- ♿ Good
- ↔ Teatro alla Scala (► 40), Museo Poldi Pezzoli (► 45), Museo Bagatti Valsecchi (► 47)

Milan is Italy's high spot for fashion and the area known as the Quadrilatero d'Oro (The Golden Quad), northeast of the Duomo, is the most exclusive shopping quarter of the city. All the top designer names are here.

Glitz and glamour The Quadrilatero d'Oro is defined by Via Montenapoleone, Via Manzoni (► 59), Via Spiga and Via Sant'Andrea. Via Manzoni is wide and traffic laden, the other streets in the shopping quarter are relatively quiet and make for pleasant shopping. Via Montenapoleone, familiarly known as Montenapo, is the most famous of these exclusive streets, lined with elegant clothing stores including Ferragamo, Armani, Valentino, Prada and Versace, and high-class jewellers.

Palaces, courtyards and museums The name Quadrilatero d'Oro comes from the early 19th century and the quarter still preserves some of its historic palazzi as well as some fascinating courtyards. Via Bigli has the oldest buildings, with some of the palaces dating back to the 17th century. The shopping district is also home to the Museo Bagatti Valsecchi (► 47) and two civic museums, both at Via Sant'Andrea 6: the Museo di Milano (► 53) and the Museo di Storia Contemporanea (Contemporary History), which is currently closed for restoration.

Milan style Don't expect a bargain unless you come during the January sales; the prices here tend to be higher than the rest of the city. The window fronts are stylish, artfully displaying the latest trends in fashion, as well as showcasing jewellery, fine leather, luxury furs and accessories, so it's a must for window-shopping and a great place to see the amazingly chic Milanese.

Museo Bagatti Valsecchi

This charming museum in a neo-Renaissance palace houses fascinating antiques and curios and an extraordinary collection of genuine and reproduction furnishings of the brothers Fausto and Giuseppe Bagatti Valsecchi.

Ardent collectors Fausto and Giuseppe Bagatti Valsecchi, born respectively in 1843 and 1845, inherited their artistic flair from their father, a famous miniaturist. Using a large team of Lombard artisans, they skilfully renovated two palazzi (one in Via Gesù, the other backing onto it in Via Santo Spirito) between 1876 and 1895, to be used as their own home. Descendants of the brothers lived here until 1974 and created the Fondazione Bagatti Valsecchi, to open the collection to the public. It is now owned by the state.

Genuine or reproduction? You can visit the brothers' private apartments and the formal rooms they shared: the drawing room, hall of arms, dining room, study and Santo Spirito atrium. The Renaissance setting can be quite convincing—as can be the reproduction furniture that is integrated with authentic pieces. No detail betrays its modernity. The piano is encased in an antique design, and even the bath and shower are concealed in a Renaissance-style marble niche. The Camera Rossa has a charming display of 15th–17th-century children's furniture, while the dining room contains tapestries, sideboards and kitchenware. The library contains a number of important and valuable 15th-century parchments. In the Valtellinese bedroom there is a wonderful 16th-century bed with finely carved scenes of *The Road to Calvary* and Old Testament scenes together with paintings by Giampietrino.

HIGHLIGHTS

- Sala dell'Affresco, named after the fresco by Antonio Boselli of the *Madonna della Misericorda* (1496)
- Library, with painted leather celestial globe
- Valtellinese Bedroom
- The Red Bedroom— Painting of *Santa Giustina de' Borromei*, Giovanni Bellini (c. 1475)

INFORMATION

- **www**.museobagattivalsecchi.org
- E2
- Via Santo Spirito 10, 20121
- 02 7600 6132
- Tue–Sun 1–5.45. Usually closed New Year's Day, 6 Jan, Easter, 25 Apr, 1 May, 15 Aug, 1 Nov, Xmas but changes each year
- Montenapoleone
- 61, 94; tram 1, 2
- None
- Expensive
- Quadrilatero d'Oro (► 46)
- Every room has detailed sheets of information, translated into 6 languages. Good guidebook

Ca' Granda

HIGHLIGHTS

- Cortile Maggiore–the spacious and elegant main courtyard with arcades surrounding the garden
- Fine 15th-century façade

INFORMATION

www.unimi.it
- D3
- Via Festa del Perdono, 5, 20122
- 02 503 111
- Mon–Fri 8–8, Sat 8–12.30
- Basic student canteen
- Missori
- 65, 77, 94; tram 12, 15
- Good
- Free
- No information or booklets

This huge building certainly lives up to its name—Casa Grande or Large House. It houses the Humanities Department of the State University and retains elegant 15th-century courtyards and the lovely baroque Cortile Maggiore.

Milan's benefactor   Otherwise known as the Ospedale Maggiore, the building was commissioned by Francesco Sforza in the mid-15th century as the main hospital in Milan, which it remained for nearly five centuries. As part of his plan to transform Milan into the ideal city, Francesco Sforza commissioned the Tuscan architect, Filarete, to build a hospital for the poor. His plans were based on a rectangle made up of ten equal squares with a church in the middle. Although Filarete's designs defined the entire building, only the right wing was constructed under the Sforzas. Guiniforte Solari (1429–91) completed Filarete's Renaissance section with the upper floor in Gothic style. In 1624, Francesco Maria Richini enlarged the hospital, and in 1797 the left wing was added. Ca' Granda was badly damaged by bombing in 1943, and owes its present-day look to post-war reconstruction and restoration, during which time it was converted to house the university.

Elegant but practical   The lengthy façade (282m/925ft) illustrates the different stages of construction from the 15th century (on the far right) through to the late 18th century. The main courtyard is the Cortile Maggiore with the Basilica dell'Annunciata opposite the entrance, and to the right are other elegant 15th-century courtyards. The hospital was very progressive for its day: Men and women were separated, sanitary services were in corridors, and the beds had built-in cupboards and folding tables.

Villa Reale and Galleria d'Arte Moderna

This vast neoclassical Royal Villa has been occupied by Napoleon and Josephine, Count Joseph Radetzky (the Austrian commander-in-chief) and the Italian royal family. Part is now home to the Gallery of Modern Art.

Former glory Today the grand central hall is a popular wedding venue for wealthy Milanese. The small building beside it is the Padiglione d'Arte Contemporanea (PAC), which hosts temporary modern art exhibitions.

Famous residents The Villa was built in 1790 by Leopold Pollack for Count Ludovico Barbiano di Belgioioso. After the count's death in the early 19th century, the Italian Government donated it as a residence for Napoleon and Josephine, and it passed into the hands of the city of Milan in 1921. PAC was rebuilt after it was destroyed in a Sicilian terrorist attack in 1993.

Modern art collection Occupying 35 rooms on the first and second floors, the gallery illustrates the main artistic movements of the 19th and early 20th century, with emphasis on Italian and French art. The large Grassi Collection has Oriental sculpture and works by Camille Corot, Paul Cézanne, Vincent Van Gogh, Henri Toulouse-Lautrec and other big names. The Museo Marino Marini opened in 1973 and contains bronzes, portrait busts and drawings by the Italian sculptor Marini (1901–80). The collection is displayed in modernized rooms with good lighting. Some of the busts depict the artist's friends and acquaintances (among them Ivor Stravinsky, Henry Miller, Henry Moore and Marc Chagall) and are remarkable for their psychological insight.

HIGHLIGHTS

- Museo Marino Marini
- *Quarto Stato* (Fourth Estate), Pelizza da Volpedo depicts the struggles and sufferings of the working classes
- Pleasant gardens

INFORMATION

- E1
- Via Palestro 16, 20121
- Galleria d'Arte Moderna: 02 8846 3731; Padiglione d'Arte Contemporanea 02 7600 9085
- Tue–Sun 9–5.30; closed 1 Jan, Easter, 1 May, 15 Aug, 25 Dec
- Palestro
- 61, 94; tram 1, 2
- Padiglione d'Arte Contemporanea good, Galleria d'Arte Moderna accessible with help
- Free
- No information or booklets

Santa Maria della Passione

The second largest church in Milan after the Duomo, it is distinctive for its handsome dome. But the main attraction is the art within the church—a gallery of 16th- and 17th-century paintings and frescoes by leading Lombard artists.

Elaborate additions Santa Maria della Passione was built in the late 14th to early 15th centuries in a Greek Cross plan and was extended with a nave and side chapels in 1573. The baroque façade, decorated with statues, was added in 1729 by Giuseppe Rusnati, who also built the adjoining convent, now the Conservatorio di Musica Giuseppe Verdi.

Artistic masterpieces The paintings and frescoes that decorate most of the church depict the Passion of Christ or similar themes. The paintings of saints perched on the piers of the nave are by Daniele Crespi. The church has numerous paintings by this Milanese master, considered the finest Lombard painter of the early 17th century. He died in his early 30s of the plague, but his output was considerable. In the first chapel on the left is Crespi's *Il Digiuno di San Carlo (The Fasting of St. Charles)*, which shows San Carlo Borromeo, Archbishop of Milan, and mastermind of the Counter-Reformation. This is Crespi's best-known work and generally regarded as the most famous 17th-century Milanese painting. It shows the saint with a loaf of bread and a carafe of water—a simple, austere composition reflecting the spirit of the Counter-Reformation.

Added bonus If you have time, peek into the Giuseppe Verdi Conservatory of Music next door to the church to see the striking courtyard.

MILAN's
best

51

Milan's Best

Museums

MUSEO DI STORIA CONTEMPORANEA

Due to re-open in 2005 after restoration, the Museum of Contemporary History (☎ 02 7600 6245) shares the Palazzo Morando Attendolo Bolognini with the Museo di Milano. It originated in 1935 as the Museo della Guerra (War Museum) within the Castello Sforzesco. The museum covers the period from 1914–45, but the main emphasis is on World War I, with paintings, sculpture, documents, diaries and other war-related memorabilia.

Milan has no shortage of museums

MUSEO DEL CINEMA

This small museum is packed with weird and wonderful magic lanterns, early 19th-century pre-camera viewers, antique snapshot cameras, early examples of cine cameras and vintage posters of Hollywood and Italian movie stars. A tiny cinema shows old films and cartoons for children at weekends.

www.cinetecamilano.it ✉ Palazzo Dugnani, Via Manin 2/b, 20121
☎ 02 655 4977 🕐 Fri–Sun 3–6 (films at 4–5; reservations essential)
🚇 Turati 🚌 61, 94; tram 1, 2 ♿ Good (narrow access path)
💶 Inexpensive

MUSEO DEL COLLEZIONISTA D'ARTE

Near the castle, this fascinating private museum shows you how to tell the difference between genuine and fake antiques. Eighteen rooms house 2,000 antiques from excavated ceramics, African art and silverware, to watches, pearls and walking sticks. You are encouraged to handle the antiques and carry out simple tests to determine the age and production techniques.

www.museodelcollezionista.com ✉ Via Q. Sella 4,
20121 ☎ 02 7202 2488 🕐 Mon–Fri 10–6, Sat 10–2
🚇 Cairoli, Lanza 🚌 57, 61; tram 1, 4, 7, 27 ♿ None
💶 Expensive; free for under 10s and over 60s

MUSEO DEL GIOCATTOLO E DEL BAMBINO (➤ 62)

MUSEO INTER & AC MILAN

This museum, Italy's first museum dedicated entirely to sport, is in the San Siro stadium, where both of Milan's soccer teams play. There are more than 3,000 items on display, including trophies, flags, soccer shirts, boots and other memorabilia relating to Milan's two famous teams Inter and AC. There are guided tours of the stadium every day except Sundays and when matches are in progress.

✉ Stadio Giuseppe Meazza (San Siro), Gate 4, Via Piccolomini 5, 20151 ☎ 02 404 2432 🕐 Daily 10–6; the museum is closed during sporting events 🚇 Lotto, then shuttle bus for matches; tram 16 ♿ Good 💵 Expensive

MUSEO DEL MANZONI

Overlooking Piazza Belgioioso in the heart of the city, this was the home of Alessandro Manzoni, considered the greatest Italian novelist of the 19th century. Born in Milan, he lived here almost continuously, from 1814 until he died in 1873. You can visit his study, library, the living rooms, 'the wedding bedroom' and the bedroom where he died.

www.museidelcentro.mi.it ✉ Via G. Morone 1 (Piazza Belgioioso), 20121 ☎ 02 8646 60403 🕐 Tue–Fri, Sun 9–12, 2–4 🚇 Duomo 🚌 61; tram 1, 2 ♿ Good 💵 Free

MUSEO DI MILANO

On the first floor of the Palazzo Morando Attendolo Bolognini, this museum is divided into two distinct parts: the Pinacoteca (Art Gallery) on the inner porticoed courtyard side, and the 18th-century apartments, which face on to Via Sant'Andrea. The Pinacoteca illustrates the changes in the city's development in the 17th to 19th centuries.

www.museidelcentro.mi.it ✉ Via Sant'Andrea 6, 20121 ☎ 02 7600 6245 🕐 Tue–Sun 9–1, 2–5.30 🚇 Montenapoleone 🚌 61, 94; tram 1, 2 ♿ Good 💵 Free

MUSEO DI STORIA NATURALE

Occupying 23 rooms of a huge mock-Romanesque late 19th-century building on the edge of the Giardini Pubblici, this museum has sections on geology, mineralogy, palaeontology, entomology, zoology and habitats. Children will be drawn to the dinosaurs and the life-size reproductions of crocodiles, snakes and sea creatures. Explanations in Italian only.

✉ Corso Venezia 55, 20121 ☎ 02 8846 3280 🕐 Tue–Sun 9–6; closed 1 Jan, 1 May, 15 Aug, Christmas 🚇 Palestro 🚌 Tram 9, 30 ♿ Few 💵 Free

MUSEO TEATRALE ALLA SCALA

The museum was founded in 1913 and has a superb collection of theatrical memorabilia. This ranges from ornate stage-curtain design, decoration for boxes, antique musical instruments, phonographs and gramophones, sketches for sets, costumes (including those for Maria Callas and Rudolf Nureyev) and the Sambon collection of paintings and ceramics. You can take a tour of the auditorium, too.

✉ Piazza della Scala, 20121 ☎ 02 469 1249 🕐 Daily 9–6, last visit 5.15). Closed 1 Jan, 1 May, 15 Aug 25–26 Dec 🚇 Duomo, Cordusio 🚌 61, tram 1, 2 ♿ Good 💵 Moderate

MUSEO DEL RISORGIMENTO

This museum is in the neoclassical Palazzo Moriggia and traces Italy's history from Napoleon's campaigns in Italy (1796 and 1800) to Unification in 1866. Exhibits include prints and paintings, original documents, busts, momentoes and proclamations. You can see the first Italian flag (Primo Tricolore), which was used at the Battle of Arcole Bridge in 1796.

www.museidelcentro.mi.it ✉ Via Borgonuovo 23, 20121 ☎ 02 8846 7170 🕐 Tue–Sun 9–1, 2–5.30 🚇 Montenapoleone 🚌 61; tram 1, 2 ♿ Good 💵 Free

53

Churches

SANTA MARIA INCORONATA

An unusual, double-fronted church in the north of the city, Santa Maria Incoronata comprises two buildings: the one on the left, built for Francesco Sforza in 1451, and the other for his wife, completed a few years later. The two were joined together in 1468. Both buildings were designed by the Gothic architect Guiniforte Solari, who built the nave of the Church of Santa Maria delle Grazie and also worked on the city's cathedral.

☒ Corso Garibaldi 116, 20121 ☎ 02 654 855 🕐 Daily 7.30–1.30 and 4–7.15 🚇 Garibaldi 🚃 94 ♿ Good 💷 Free

SAN FEDELE

This is popular with the Milanese and one of the city's finest examples of baroque architecture. The church was commissioned by San Carlo Borromeo in 1569, archbishop of Milan and a leading player during the Counter-Reformation. The elaborate façade is decorated with reliefs on the pediment and sculpted figures in the niches. Although internally less exciting, the church has some beautifully carved wooden furniture.

☒ Piazza Fedele, 20121 ☎ 02 7200 8027 🕐 Daily 8.30–2.30, 4–7 🚇 Duomo 🚃 61; tram 1, 2 ♿ Poor; seven steps up to church 💷 Free

SAN MARCO

Built in 1254, the present church was founded on the site of the 12th-century church of San Marco. It was designed in Romanesque style, but underwent major Gothic and baroque transformations—plus some heavy-handed 19th-century restoration. The main portal with bas-reliefs and the tower with decorative friezes (only seen from Via Pontaccio) survive from the 13th-century church.

☒ Piazza San Marco 2, 20121 ☎ 02 2900 2598 🕐 Daily 7.30–11, 4–7 🚃 61, 43 ♿ Few 💷 Free

SAN NAZARO MAGGIORE

Sant'Ambrogio, the bishop of Milan, built this church in the late fourth century to shelter the remains of apostles Andrew, John and Thomas. Ten years later, he discovered the remains of San Nazaro near by and dedicated his church to the saint. The main church is

Madonna and Child *from over the door of the church of San Marco*

reached via the beautiful octagonal Trivulzio chapel.
✉ Piazza San Nazaro, 20122 ☎ 02 5830 7719 🕐 Daily 7.30–12,
3–6.30 🚍 77, 94; tram 4, 16 ♿ Good 🎟 Free

SAN PIETRO IN GESSATE

The church was originally designed by the eminent
Gothic architect Guiniforte Solari, but underwent
major transformations over the centuries and
subsequently suffered bomb damage in 1943. It is a
delightful church, with some remarkable frescoes.
✉ Piazza San Pietro in Gessate, 20122 ☎ 02 545 0145 🕐 Daily
7.30–6 🚍 60; tram 12, 23, 27 ♿ Good 🎟 Free

SAN SIMPLICIANO

This handsome basilica, flanking a square that is
otherwise occupied by dreary modern blocks, is the
finest of the churches in the Brera quarter. It was
founded in the fourth century, possibly by
Sant'Ambrogio, and reconstructed in the 12th
century. Don't miss the enchanting fresco in the apse
by Bergognone of the *Coronation of the Virgin* (c. 1515).
✉ Piazza San Simpliciano 7, 20121 ☎ 02 862 274
🕐 Mon–Sat 7.10–12, 3–7; Sun 7.30–12.30, 4–7
Ⓜ Lanza 🚍 57, 61; tram 12, 14 ♿ Good 🎟 Free

SANTA MARIA PRESSO SAN CELSO

Legend has it that in the 4th century,
Sant'Ambrogio discovered the remains of
two martyrs, Nazaro and Celso, where San
Celso stands today. This small Romanesque
church was built in AD996 to protect an
image of the Madonna of Sant'Ambrogio
that was discovered nearby. The adjacent
basilica of Santa Maria dei Miracoli (1493)
was named after the Madonna and the faded
remains of the venerated fresco survive on
the altar.
✉ Corso Italia 37, 20122 ☎ 02 5831 3187 (Santa Maria
dei Miracoli) 🕐 Santa Maria dei Miracoli daily 7–12,
4–7.30; San Celso opens only for exhibitions and concerts
Ⓜ Garibaldi 🚍 94 ♿ Good 🎟 Free

SANT'ANGELO

This splendid church was built in 1554 to replace an
older Franciscan church that was outside the city walls
and therefore in danger of attack. The present church
underwent major restoration in the last century, the
convent was rebuilt, and the prestigious Franciscan
Library reopened. The church has several 16th- and
17th-century works of art by leading Lombard
painters.
✉ Piazza Sant'Angelo 2, 20121 🕐 Mon–Fri 6.30am–8pm, Sat
6.30–12, 3.30–8, Sun 8–1, 3.30–8 Ⓜ Turati 🚍 43, 94 ♿ Good
🎟 Free

CHURCH ETIQUETTE

The Roman Catholic Church
still plays a dominant role in
Italian life. Always dress with
respect for Italian sensibilities
when entering Milan's
churches. Don't wear mini
skirts or shorts and cover up
bare shoulders. If you do
happen to go into a church
when a service is in progress–
which you should try to
avoid–be as inconspicuous as
possible.

*The austere beauty of
San Simpliciano*

Palazzos

PALAZZO CASTIGLIONI

You can't miss this vast, dark grey, art nouveau palace, built in 1901–04 by Giuseppe Sommaruga. The putti and swags decorating the façade between the second and third floors lend light relief. Two female nudes that used to flank the portal caused outrage and were removed to the garden of Villa Romeo-Faccanoni, today the Clinico Columbus. The nudes gave the palace its nickname of Ca' di Ciapp (House of the Buttocks).

✉ Corso Venezia 47, 20121 🕐 View from outside only 🚇 Palestro 🚌 61, 94

PALAZZO FONTANA-SILVESTRI

The oldest and most beautiful building along the Corso Venezia, the Renaissance palace stands incongruously between modern blocks at the San Babila end of the street. Corso Venezia was formerly called Corso di Porta Orientale, taking its name from the gate.

✉ Corso Venezia 10, 20121 🕐 View from outside only 🚇 San Babila 🚌 54, 60, 61

PALAZZO DI GIUSTIZIA

Opposite the lovely church of San Pietro in Gessate (► 54), this palace is a vast monument to Fascism. Home to Milan's Law Courts, it replaced the old Tribunale in Piazza Beccaria near the Duomo. The building, with over 1,000 rooms and 65 law courts, was designed by Marcello Piacentini in the 1930s.

✉ Corso di Porta Vittoria, 20122 🕐 View from outside only 🚇 San Babila 🚌 60; tram 12, 23 27

The statue of Leonardo da Vinci, outside Palazzo Marino in Piazza della Scala

PALAZZO LITTA

The majestic late baroque façade of Palazzo Litta dominates this stretch of Corso Magenta. The interior, with its splendid Salone degli Specchi (Hall of Mirrors) and other opulent rooms, can only be visited when special events are held here. You can peek into the porticoed Cortile d'Onore (Courtyard of Honour) during office hours.

✉ Corso Magenta 24, 20123 ☎ Information from APT (tourist information) 02 7740 2973 ⏱ Only open for special events 🚇 Cadorna 🚌 50, 58; tram 19, 24

PALAZZO MARINO

On the same square as Teatro alla Scala, this is an imposing baroque palace with a late 19th-century façade. It was built in 1558 for Tommaso Marino, a wealthy Genoese financier, and since 1860 it has been the city's Town Hall. The palace is not open to the public, but don't miss the porticoed Courtyard of Honour, which can be glimpsed from Via Marina (to the right as you face the façade).

✉ Piazza della Scala, 20121 ⏱ View from outside only 🚇 Duomo, Cordusio 🚌 61; tram 1, 2

PALLAZZO DELLA RAGIONE

A splendid red-brick medieval building, with rounded arches and a ground-floor loggia that dominates Piazza Mercanti (➤ 39). It was built in 1233 by the *podestà* (governor), Oldrado da Tresseno, who is depicted in an equestrian relief on the side facing the square.

✉ Piazza Mercanti, 20123 ⏱ View from outside only 🚇 Duomo 🚌 Tram 2, 3, 15, 24

PALAZZO DEL SENATO

Home to the State Archives since 1872, this imposing baroque palazzo was built in 1608 on the site of a seminary. During the Napoleonic era, it became the seat of the Senate.

✉ Via Senato 10, 20121 ⏱ View from outside only 🚇 Montenapoleone, Palestro 🚌 61, 94

PALAZZO SERBELLONI

This monumental neoclassical palace has played host to famous historical figures such as Napoleon and Josephine, King Vittorio Emanuele II and the Austrian statesman Metternich, among others. It was built in 1793, and was partially restored after the bombings in World War II. During office hours, you can walk through the huge arched entrance to the frescoed loggia and arcaded courtyard—now used for parking.

✉ Corso Venezia, 16, 20121 ⏱ View from outside only 🚇 San Babila 🚌 61

Streets & Piazzas

PIAZZA DUOMO

Throbbing with activity, this is the heart of historic Milan. A cross-section of society gathers here in front of the soaring Duomo, which dominates the piazza. The square was designed in 1865, and on the north side is the Galleria Vittorio Emanuele II, the first iron and glass construction of its kind in Italy (➤ 44). The imposing equestrian statue of the king at the western end of the piazza was unveiled in 1896.

CORSO MATTEOTTI

A wide, traffic-choked street linking Piazza Meda with Piazza San Babila. It was built in the 1930s and is representative of Fascist architecture. There are some trendy design shops and the beautifully preserved Café Sant'Ambroeus, at No. 7 (➤ 71), whose cakes are hard to resist.
🚇 San Babila, 🚌 61

CORSO DI PORTA ROMANA

The ancient route to Rome started at the Porta Romana (Roman Gate). One of the city's busiest streets, it is lined with small shops, *pasticcerie* and cafés. The buildings of architectural interest, neoclassical and flamboyant art nouveau *palazzi*, lie towards the Piazza Missori end.
✉ 20121 🚇 Missori, Crocetta, Porta Romana 🚌 77; tram 24

CORSO VENEZIA

This wide traffic-laden artery linking Piazza San Babila to Piazza Oberdan, was a relatively quiet area with trees and gardens prior to the mid-18th century. The street now has a splendid array of *palazzi*, from Renaissance to neoclassical and art nouveau.
✉ 20122 🚇 San Babila, Palestro 🚌 60

CORSO VITTORIO EMANUELE II

Linking Piazza del Duomo and Piazza San Babila, this is the city's main shopping street. It's a wide pedestrian thoroughfare lined with arcades, galleries, cafés and late-night bars. Less chic and more lively than the Quadrilatero d'Oro to the north, it attracts a younger crowd.
✉ 20121 🚇 Duomo, San Babila 🚌 61, 65, 73; tram 23

PIAZZA SAN BABILA

A rendezvous point for young Milanese. In the northwest corner is the pretty church of San Babila; the best views are from the far corner of the square.
✉ 20122 🚇 San Babila 🚌 54, 61

VIA BRERA

The Brera is one of the oldest and most attractive districts in Milan. For many years this quarter was inhabited by artists and there is still a hint of Bohemia. Via Brera is its liveliest street, popular with the young for its open-air cafés, inviting *trattorie*, galleries, street vendors and late-night bars.
✉ 20121 🚌 61; tram 1, 27

VIA BROLETTO

The street runs north from Piazza Cordusio, where part of the old city was demolished in the late 19th century to make way for a new financial district. Banks, the post office and the Assicurazioni Generali building (designed by Luca Beltrami) surround the piazza.

✉ 20121 🚇 Cordusio 🚋 Tram 1, 3, 12, 27

VIA DANTE

Linking Largo Cairoli to Castello Sforzesco, this pedestrian thoroughfare was built at the end of the 19th century as part of a major scheme to revamp the northwest into a smart residential/business quarter. Alfresco cafés spill out onto the street, and elegant shops occupy the lower floors of fine neoclassical buildings. The northwest end of the street is dominated by an equestrian statue of Garibaldi in the Largo Cairoli and beyond it is the soaring clock tower of the Castello.

✉ 20121 🚇 Cordusio, Cairoli 🚋 18, 50, 58; tram 19, 24 and others

VIA MANZONI

This fashionable shopping street, which links Piazza della Scala with Piazza Cavour, forms the west side of the Quadrilatero d'Oro (▶ 46). The ground floors of its imposing *palazzi* are devoted to stylish designer stores with tantalizing window displays. Since it opened in 1863, the Grand Hotel et de Milan (No. 29) has played host to royalty, politicans and famous artists including Verdi, who stayed here from 1887 until his death in 1901.

✉ 20121 🚇 Montenapoleone 🚋 61, 94; tram 1, 2

VIA TORINO

Linking the middle of the city to the Ticinese quarter, this is one of the busiest streets of central Milan, with a constant rattle of trams. The main attractions are the fashion shops and Bramante's beautiful church of Santa Maria presso San Satiro (▶ 38).

✉ 20123 🚇 Duomo 🚋 Tram 2, 3, 14

CORSO PORTA TICINESE

This street ends at one of the remaining medieval gates surrounding the heart of Milan: Porta Ticinese. This area is becoming popular with younger shoppers as the trendy, retro clothing and accessory boutiques are less expensive than the designer shops farther north. Its bohemian atmosphere makes it a fun shopping experience and it also has several good traditional *trattorie*.

There is a fine view of the Castello's clock tower from the outdoor cafés in Via Dante

Buildings & Monuments

ARENA CIVICA

This huge amphitheatre was built in 1806 by Luigi Canonica to seat 30,000 spectators. Entertainment took the form of chariot races, shows and – when filled with water from the Navigli canals – mock naval battles. It has since hosted soccer games and pop concerts; today it is mainly used for athletic events.
✉ North end of Via Manzoni, Via Comizi di Lioni 1, Parco Sempione, 20154 🕐 Open for events only Ⓜ Lanza 🚌 57, 70; tram 3, 4, 12, 14

The Bastioni at Porta Venezia

ARCHI DI PORTA NUOVA

The large, double-arched gateway separates Via Manzoni and Piazza Cavour. This and Porta Ticinese are the only surviving gates of the medieval walls that protected the city.
✉ North end of Via Manzoni, 20121 Ⓜ Montenapoleone 🚌 61, 94; tram 1, 2

BASTIONI DI PORTA VENEZIA

On the site of one of the Porte Regie (Royal Gates) in the Spanish city walls, constructed in the 16th century, the present-day triumphal arch dates from 1828.
✉ Piazza Oberdan, 20129 Ⓜ Porta Venezia 🚌 Tram 9, 29, 30

CIMITERO MONUMENTALE

The neo-Romanesque cemetery (1866) covers an area of 250,000sq m (900,000sq ft) in the northwest of the city. Eminent Milanese and other Italians, including novelist Manzoni and the poet Salvatore Quasimodo, are buried in the focal Famae Aedes (House of Fame). Some fine monumental sculpture.
✉ North end of Via Manzoni, 20154 Piazzale Cimitero Monumentale ☎ 02 659 9938 🕐 Tue–Fri 8.30–5.14, Sat–Sun 8.30–5.45 🚌 41, 70, 94; tram 14 ♿ Good

EDIFICIO PIRELLI

Familiarly known as Pirellone or Big Pirelli, Milan's highest skyscraper (127m/417ft), was completed in 1960. It was designed by Gio Ponti and Pier Luigi Nervi, and is now occupied by the Lombardy regional council.
✉ Piazza Duca d'Aosta/Via G.B. Pirelli, 20124 🕐 View from outside only 🚌 42, 60, 82; tram 2, 5, 9, 20, 33

STAZIONE CENTRALE

Stazione Centrale is not just Milan's main railway station. It is the biggest in Italy and is a majestic building that commands great respect architecturally. Although it was not completed until 1931 it was designed in 1912 and its style is more characteristic of the art nouveau movement than the heavy Fascist architecture of the 1930s.
✉ Piazzale Duca d'Aosta, 20124 🕐 24 hours, tourist information Mon–Sat 9–6.30, Sun 9–12.30, 1.30–5 Ⓜ Centrale 🚌 42, 60, 82, 92; tram 2, 5, 33 ♿ Good

Parks, Gardens & Canals

In the Top 25
❹ PARCO SEMPIONE (► 29)

GIARDINO DELLA GUASTALLA
The oldest public garden in Milan was founded in 1555 by Paola Ludovica Torelli, Countess of Guastalla, who planned it as part of the Guastalla College for daughters of impoverished local nobles. There are several monuments and a fish pond.
✉ Via San Barnaba, 20122 🕐 Daily 8–4 (longer hours in summer)
🚌 60, 77; tram 12, 27

GIARDINI PUBBLICI
The largest gardens in Milan, created in 1782 on the lines of an English park and extended in the 19th century. The various attractions include the Natural History Museum, Planetarium and Cinema Museum, along with summer entertainment in the form of donkey rides, mini-train rides and a merry-go-round
✉ Northwest of city, 20121 🕐 Daily 6.30am–sunset Ⓜ Turati, Palestro, Porta Venezia, Repubblica 🚌 94; tram 1, 2, 29, 30

NAVIGLI
In the southwest of the city, this quarter is named after the navigable canals that were important trade routes for barges. Barge transport ceased completely in 1979 and the Navigli, a working class quarter, has become a popular arty district with restaurants and nightlife, antique workshops and galleries. Canal cruises are organized from June to September.
✉ West of Piazza XXIV Maggio, 20123 Ⓜ Porta Genova 🚌 59; tram 2, 3 💰 Canal cruises expensive

PARCO DELLE BASILICHE
Named after the basilicas of San Lorenzo and Sant'Eustorgio, this is a pleasant park in the southeast of the city. A pathway flanked by roses links the two basilicas—with the busy Via Molino delle Armi in between. Formerly this was one of the least desirable spots in the city where public hangings took place and tanners' workshops created a foul stench. Fortunately, it now affords a more pleasurable experience.
✉ Southeast of city, 20123 🚌 94; tram 3

PARCO LAMBRO
This large park (over 90ha/222 acres) to the east of the city is a good place to relax and escape the heat and noise of Milan in high summer. It was designed to mirror the natural Lombardy countryside with the River Lambro meandering through the middle and has numerous small lakes and ponds. Team sports and rowing are popular activities here.
✉ East of city Ⓜ Udine 🚌 55

NOT SO GREEN

Milan is not a city graced with a large amount of green space. In summer, most Milanese head out to the lakes or mountains to avoid the stifling heat. However, don't despair if you are in the city when it's hot as there are several parks (see this page), peaceful church and palace gardens and the canals to escape to. You can be in the country in no time by taking advantage of the efficient public transport system.

Attractions at the Giardini Pubblici include a children's play area

For Children

In the Top 25
---
1 MUSEO NAZIONALE DELLA SCIENZA E DELLA TECNICA (► 26)
4 PARCO SEMPIONE (► 29)

FARTHER AFIELD

Milan is probably not the ideal city to bring children. But if you have a car and are prepared to travel you will find several attractions to keep them happy not too far outside the city. Within the city the best bets for children are the sports facilities and swimming pools, ice-skating at Palazzo del Ghiaccio (✉ Via Piranesi ☎ 02 73981), or they can run off steam in one of the parks. A highlight of many a child's trip to Milan would be a visit to the San Siro soccer stadium.

Child-size transport in Giardini Pubblici

AQUATICA

A great family day out in the suburbs at San Siro, this water park has pools, thrilling slides, fountains, tubes, river rides and some artificial beaches for relaxing.
www.parcoaquatica.com ✉ Via G Airaghi 61, 20153 ☎ 02 4820 0134 🕐 Daily 10–7, Jun–Aug 🚇 De Angeli then bus 72, Primaticcio then bus 64, Lotto then bus 423 💶 Expensive

GARDALAND

With over 38 exciting attractions and rides to chose from, plus lots of theme shops and restaurants, it is well worth the trip to this park, 50km (31 miles) east of the city. Highlights include Fantasy Kingdom, Magic Mountain, Blue Tornado and Atlantide.
www.gardaland.it ✉ Viale Gadio 2, 37014 ☎ 045 644 9777 🕐 Daily 9.30–6, late Mar–mid–Jun; daily 9am–midnight, mid Jun–mid Sep; Sat–Sun 9.30–6, Oct 🚇 Stazione Centrale, Milan to Peschiera del Garda, then free shuttle bus to park 💶 Expensive

MUSEO DEL GIOCATTOLO E DEL BAMBINO

A huge toy museum about 3km (2 miles) west of the city. Displays include 18th-century handcrafted toys, tin science-fiction toys and papier-mâché dolls from the 1950s and 60s. Exhibits take on various themes such as Pinocchio, the Golden Age of the Toy (1880–1915), the theatre and circus.
www.museodelgiocattolo.it ✉ Via Pitteri 56, 20134 ☎ 02 2641 1585 🕐 Tue–Sun 9.30–12.30, 3–6 🚇 Lambrate, then bus 54, 75 ♿ Good 💶 Moderate

PLANETARIO ULRICO HOEPLI

On the eastern edge of the Giardini Pubblici, Italy's biggest planetarium has a domed projection room with a capacity for 300. Themes change monthly—check the website or ask at the tourist office.
www.brera.mi.astro.it ✉ Corso Venezia 57, 20121 ☎ 02 2953 1181 🕐 Tue and Thu 9pm, Sat and Sun 3pm and 4.30pm 🚇 Porta Venezia 🚊 Tram 9, 29, 30 ♿ Good 💶 Moderate

PARCO DELLA PREISTORIA

Parco della Preistoria is 25km (16 miles) east of central Milan at Rivolta d'Adda. It has over 20 reconstructions of prehistoric animals scattered throughout woodland and along the river. Also play areas, a restaurant, picnic areas and train rides.
www.parcodellapreistoria.it ✉ Via Ponte Vecchia 21, Rivolta d'Adda (take A7 Milano–Genova highway, exit Linate, then follow to Rivolta) ☎ 0376 78184/370 250 🕐 Daily 9–7, mid Feb–early Nov ♿ Good 💶 Expensive

MILAN
where to...

Elegant/Trendy

PRICES

Expect to pay per person for a meal, excluding drinks

€   =   Up to €20
€€   =   €20– €50
€€€   =   Over €50

KING OF DESIGN

Fashion designer Roberto Cavalli is a household name in Milan renowned for his chain of clothing stores, but he is not just famous for his catwalk styles. He also owns the Milanese hot spot the Just Cavalli Café, in the Parco Sempione at the base of the Torre Branca. The semi-circular steel and glass structure encloses a sophisticated restaurant with lime green sofas, African-style accessories and a formal dining area. Here you can sip cocktails with celebrities and choose dishes from worldwide cuisines such as coriander and onion marmalade, noodles with olives, and basmati rice with Mediterranean seafood. Garden, complete with gazebo. ✉ Viale Luigi Cameons, Torre Branca, 20121 ☎ 02 311 817 🕐 Mon–Sat dinner, Sun lunch only 🚇 Cadorna

AIMO E NADIA €€€

Central Italian cuisine, cooked by award-winning chef Signor Aimo and his wife, Nadia. Every dish is a masterpiece, served in intimate surroundings. ✉ Via Montecuccoli 6, 20147 ☎ 02 416 886 🕐 Mon–Fri lunch, dinner; Sat dinner only 🚇 Primaticcio

BICE €€

Founded in 1926, Bice is in one of the smartest streets in the fashion district and is popular with the Milanese élite. Extensive à la carte menu; lighter set menu for lunch. ✉ Via Borgospesso 12, 20121 ☎ 02 7600 2572 🕐 Mon–Sat lunch, dinner 🚇 Montenapoleone

CHANDELIER €€

Real innovative fare made from a simple fusion of quality, fresh ingredients. Bright young things and arty types make up the majority of the clientele. ✉ Via Broggi Giuseppe 17, 20129 ☎ 02 2024 0458 🕐 Tue–Sat dinner only 🚇 Lima

GIANNINO €€€

Sophisticated and expensive, Giannino's has been in business for over 100 years. Top cuisine and a very large menu, which includes excellent seafood and wonderful desserts. Good wine list; lovely garden. ✉ Via A. Sciesa 8, 20135 ☎ 02 5519 5582 🕐 Tue–Sat lunch, dinner; Mon dinner only 🚇 San Babila

IL SAMBUCO €€€

One of the best restaurants in Milan, in the elegant Hermitage Hotel (► 86) in the north of the city. Fish and seafood are among the house specials, but it is equally renowned for its steak and its regional dishes. ✉ Via Messina 10, 20154 ☎ 02 3361 0333 🕐 Mon–Fri lunch, dinner; Sat dinner only 🚇 Garibaldi 🚊 Tram 14

SANTINI €€€

This is the epitome of sophistication with cool, clean lines and modern lighting. The striking blue-and-white dining room is very distinctive. A full menu features fusion and Piedmont cuisine or there are light lunch options such as spaghetti or vegetable wraps. Covered garden area for alfresco eating. ✉ Via San Marco, 20121 ☎ 02 655 5587 🕐 Mon–Fri lunch, dinner; Sat lunch only 🚇 Lanza

SAVINI €€€

Legendary Milanese restaurant that has been serving food since 1867, especially to the rich and famous visiting Teatro alla Scala. The well-prepared food, based on the finest ingredients, lives up to the best Milanese traditions. ✉ Galleria Vittorio Emanuele II, 20122 ☎ 02 7200 3433 🕐 Mon–Sat lunch, dinner. Closed 3 weeks Aug 🚇 Duomo

Milanese/Italian

AL MERCANTE €€

Eat outside in summer at this restaurant in one of the most attractive medieval squares in Milan. Tasty pasta, meat and fish dishes, and a good wine list.

✉ Piazza Mercanti 17, 20123
☎ 02 805 2198
🕐 Mon–Sat lunch, dinner
🚇 Duomo, Cordusio

ARTUROAS LA LATTERIA €–€€

Busy family-run restaurant serving food from the Lombardy region. Often frequented by journalists and the occasional celebrity.

✉ Via San Marco 24, 20121
☎ 02 659 7653
🕐 Mon–Fri lunch, dinner
🚇 Moscova

CANTINA DELLA VETRA €€

One of the few top-drawer real Italian restaurants, close to the Porta Ticinese and the San Lorenzo ruins. Giant slabs of lasagne, stew, hearty pastas and grilled meats.

✉ Piazza Vetra 5
☎ 02 894 0384 🕐 Mon–Sat lunch, dinner; Sun dinner only
🚇 Sant'Ambrogio

CRACCO PECK €€€

Modern Italian cuisine cooked with the finest and freshest ingredients have given Carlo Cracco's restaurant an international reputation. Reservations advised.

✉ Via Victor Hugo 4, 20123
☎ 02 876 774
🕐 Mon–Fri lunch, dinner; Sat dinner only. Closed Aug
🚇 Duomo

EL BRELLÍN €€

Atmospheric restaurant in an attractive former grocery and wash-house beside the canal. Typical Milanese cooking and good wine list. Try the Sunday brunch.

✉ Alzaia Naviglio Grande 14, 20144 ☎ 02 5810 1351
🕐 Mon–Sat lunch, dinner; Sun brunch only 🚇 Porta Genova

MAURO IL BOLOGNESE €€

A wealth of dishes from Bologna, the city known to Italians as 'the fat' for its wonderful, rich food. Every dish bursts with seasonal delights, such as mushrooms, truffles, soft fruit or tomatoes.

✉ Via Lombardini 14, 20143
☎ 02 837 2866
🕐 Tue–Sun lunch, dinner
🚇 Romolo

ORIENT EXPRESS €€€

In one of the most picturesque streets in the Brera district, this restaurant recreates scenes from the Orient Express; first-class dining in the intimate luxury of a railway carriage.

✉ Via Fiori Chiari 8, 20121
☎ 02 805 6227 🕐 Mon–Sat lunch, dinner; Sun brunch only
🚇 Lanza

SOLFERINO €€

One of the oldest restaurants in the city, which serves excellent Milanese dishes in beautiful surroundings.

✉ Via Castelfidardo 2, 20121
☎ 02 2900 5748 🕐 Mon–Fri lunch, dinner; Sat, Sun dinner only 🚇 Moscova

MILANESE COOKING

The cuisine of Milan and the Lombardy region has a long tradition and remains popular today. Dishes that appear on most menus include the *risotto allo zafferano*, (rice cooked with saffron), minestrone soup, *polenta pasticciata* (polenta pie with cheese sauce and white truffles), *costoletta alla milanese* (breaded veal cutlet), *osso buco alla milanese* (veal stewed with the marrow bone) and *rostin negaa* (veal chops in white wine).

Fish/Seafood/Vegetarian

REGIONAL FISH DISHES

Although Milan does not have a typical Lombardy cuisine, it has embraced the cooking of the surrounding area. The fish market in Milan is one of the finest in Italy, and you will find the freshest fish and seafood on many restaurant menus. A visit to the lakes gives you the chance to sample some good local fish such as carp or tench, while the restaurants in the areas close to the River Po serve eel and catfish.

10 CORSO COMO CAFFE €€

The vegetarian options are popular at this trendy store's café. Organic Mediterranean and Japanese food, served in elegant surroundings.
✉ Corso Como 10, 20154
☎ 02 2901 3581 🕐 Tue–Sun lunch, dinner; Mon dinner only
Ⓜ Garibaldi

ASSO DI FIORI €€

Attractive traditional restaurant by the canal, dedicated to cheese, cheese and more cheese! Delicious desserts, too.
✉ Alzaia Naviglio Grande 54, 20144 ☎ 02 8940 9415
🕐 Mon–Fri lunch, dinner; Sat dinner only Ⓜ Porta Genova

LA BONACCIA €€–€€€

Everything is nautical at this excellent fish restaurant where you can dine in a submarine with the stars twinkling above. Try the sushi.
✉ Via Marghera 22, 20129
☎ 02 498 4676 🕐 Daily lunch, dinner Ⓜ De Angeli

IL CONSOLARE €€

Airy, bright restaurant that focuses on fish; try the orata (sea bream). Popular with locals
✉ Via Ciovasso 3, 20121 ☎ 02 805 3581 🕐 Wed–Sat lunch, dinner; Tue dinner only
Ⓜ Cairoli, Lanza

LA COZZERIA €

Each dish here is based upon a kilogram (about 2lb) of mussels. Chefs curry them, pepper them, make them into a soup or serve them with cream, spices or liqueurs.

✉ Via Muratori 7, 20135
☎ 02 5410 7164 🕐 Tue–Sun lunch, dinner; Mon dinner only
Ⓜ Porta Romana

DA GASPARE €€

Despite refreshingly low prices, Da Gaspare stands head and shoulders above the rest of Milan's fish restaurants. Small, uncomfortable and often noisy, but the regulars keep flooding back.
✉ Via Correggio 39, 20149
☎ 02 4800 6409 🕐 Thu–Tue lunch, dinner Ⓜ Buonarroti

JOIA €€€

Closeness to nature is the philosophy behind this first-class vegetarian restaurant. In elegant surroundings, the freshest of ingredients are lovingly prepared to tempt the palate.
✉ Via P. Castaldi 18, 20124
☎ 02 2952 2124 🕐 Mon–Sat lunch, dinner. Closed 3 weeks Aug
Ⓜ Repubblica, Porta Venezia

LA TERRAZZA €€

Eat sushi on the top floor of this office block while taking in the great view over the Giardini Pubblici. Rooftop terrace open in summer.
✉ Via Palesto 2, 20121 ☎ 02 7600 2186 🕐 Tue–Sat lunch, dinner; Mon dinner only Ⓜ Lotto

TOM E SABATINO €€

Trendy eatery some way out of the city. Raw fish, oysters, carpaccios of both salmon and tuna, sea anemones and sponges are served with cream and fresh bread.
✉ Via De Angelis 13, 20100
☎ 02 7000 4621 🕐 Mon–Fri lunch, dinner; Sat dinner only
Ⓜ Lotto

International Cuisines

COPACABANA €€€

Milan's only dedicated Brazilian restaurant, with a Copacabana atmosphere. Giant ribs, steaks, oxtail and thick stews are served with black beans, spicy rice and salads.
✉ Via Tartini 13, 20122 ☎ 02 3931 3142 ⏰ Tue–Sun dinner only Ⓜ Repubblica; then trolleybus 82 in the direction of Via Giovan Battista Varè. Stop at Via Tartini

LOCANDO GRECO €€

Milan's oldest Greek restaurant overlooks a canal. Traditional dishes, such as *tzatziki* and *moussaka*, well prepared.
✉ Via Ripa Ticinese 69, 20143 ☎ 02 5810 1834 ⏰ Mon–Sat dinner only Ⓜ Porta Genova

NOBU €€€

Chef Nobuyuki Matsuhisa has been creating culinary treats for over 10 years in the Armani store. Here Japanese cuisine meets South American and Californian influences. Very smart and very expensive.
✉ Via Manzoni 31, 20121 ☎ 02 6231 2645 ⏰ Tue–Sat lunch, dinner; Mon dinner only Ⓜ Montenapoleone

RANGOLI €

Authentic North Indian cuisine in the Brera district. The dishes cooked in the *tandoor* (clay oven) are particularly popular. Vegetarian menu.
✉ Via Solferino 36, 20121 ☎ 02 2900 5333 ⏰ Mon–Fri lunch, dinner; Sat dinner only Ⓜ Moscova

SHANGRI-LA €€

Spicy Thai and traditional Chinese cooking. For something a little different try the fried rice served in half a pineapple.
✉ Via Lazzaretto 8, 20124 ☎ 02 2951 0837 ⏰ Wed–Mon lunch, dinner Ⓜ Repubblica, Porta Venezia

SPICE €

For a change from pizza and pasta, try this Thai restaurant a little north-east of the city.
✉ Via Ippolito Nievo 33, 20145 ☎ 02 341 290 ⏰ Mon–Sat lunch, dinner Ⓜ Pagano, Buonarroti

TANDUR €€

First-class Indian fare right in the *centro storico*. Tandur specializes in tandoori dishes.
✉ Via Maddalena 3, 20122 ☎ 02 805 6192 ⏰ Tue–Sun lunch, dinner Ⓜ Missori

UNCO €–€€

The name is short for Unconventional Restaurant, and so it is! Small morsels of a host of international tastes— from India to Mexico, Japan to South America.
✉ Via Pavia 8, 20143 ☎ 02 5810 8230 ⏰ Mon–Sat lunch, dinner Ⓜ Porta Genova

YAR €€€

Milan's only dedicated Russian restaurant. Pricey, but the fixed-price menu is cheaper. Dried smoked fish, *borsht* and deer steak.
✉ Via Mercalli Giuseppe 22, 20122 ☎ 02 5830 5234 ⏰ Mon-Sat dinner only Ⓜ Missori

ETHNIC VARIETY

It has taken some years for international and ethnic cuisine to take hold in Milan—despite the fact that large numbers of immigrants moved to the city for work during the economic expansion of the 1980s. The Milanese have remained loyal to the traditional Italian cuisine, but gradually a more cosmopolitan attitude to food is coming to the fore. You can find fine restaurants cooking up dishes from Asia, South America and North Africa.

67

Trattorias & Osterias

TRATTORIA OR OSTERIA?

In general, a *trattoria* is an unpretentious, family-run concern often with a regular clientele of local people who drop in when they do not want to cook for themselves. *Osteria* used to be the most basic of all, where simple dishes were washed down with jugs of local wine. But beware: recently the name has been adopted by some of the most expensive or touristy establishments. You can usually follow the guidelines that the smarter the premises, the more expensive the restaurant.

AL PONT DE FERR €–€€
Traditional *osteria* with brick archways and heavy wood panelling. Try the vegetable crêpes with cheese.
Ripa di Porta Ticinese 55, 20143 ☎ 02 8940 6277
Daily lunch, dinner
Porta Genova

C'ERA UNA VOLTA €€
The atmosphere at this *trattoria* changes with the time of day: Lunch is relaxed, loud and crowded with office workers; for dinner it's tablecloths, candles and couples sharing a romantic meal. Good pasta and fish dishes.
Via Palermo 20, 20121
☎ 02 654 060
Mon–Sat lunch, dinner
Moscova

OSTERIA DEI BINARI €€
In summer you can eat outside in one of the nicest gardens in Milan. This osteria specializes in dishes from Lombardy and Piedmont. Friendly service.
Via Tortona 1, 20144
☎ 02 8940 6753
Mon–Sat dinner only
Porta Genova

PONTE ROSSO €€
Not your typical *trattoria*—this one is smart with a trendy orange and black interior, and looks more like a French bistro. Simple home-cooked Italian food like *mamma* used to make.
Ripa di Porta Ticinese 23, 20143 ☎ 02 837 3132
Tue–Sat lunch, dinner; Mon dinner only Porta Genova

TRATTORIA ALL'ANTICA €–€€
Memorable Milanese and Lombard cuisine. Small and very popular, so reserve in advance.
Via Montevideo 4, 20144
☎ 02 5810 4360 Mon–Fri lunch, dinner, Sat dinner only
Sant'Agostino

TRATTORIA MILANESE €€
For a taste of old Milan, come to this tiny *trattoria* in the heart of the city. In business for a century, the trattoria reflects the past and the excellent food lives up to the Milanese tradition.
Via Santa Marta 11, 20123
☎ 02 8645 1991
Wed–Mon lunch, dinner
Cordusio, Missori

VECCHIA CANONICA €€
The eye-catching bright yellow-and-green façade draws you to this intimate *trattoria* and pizzeria. Inside, the artexed white walls and pink tablecloths give a simpler impression. The food is attractively presented.
Via Rosimi 1/b, 20154
☎ 02 349 4401 Thu–Tue lunch, dinner Moscova

LE VIGNE €€
There is lots of hustle and bustle at this rustic *osteria* on the canalside. It does get very crowded but it's worth waiting for a table to sample the excellent food, especially the stews.
Ripa di porta Ticinese 61, 20143 ☎ 02 837 5617
Mon–Sat lunch, dinner
Porta Genova

Pizzeria

BE BOP €
Pizza with nice thin, crispy bases. For those wanting something else there's also a selection of pasta, salads and snacks.
✉ Viale Col di Lana 4, 20136
☎ 02 837 6972 🕐 All day
Ⓜ Porta Genova

CHARLESTON €
In the heart of the shopping and theatre area, serving a wide variety of pizza plus some interesting Florentine dishes as well. Dine under the gazebo in summer.
✉ Plazza del Liberty 8, 20121
☎ 02 798 631
🕐 Tue–Sat all day Ⓜ Duomo, San Babila

DAI DAMM II €
Excellent spot for lunch and a rest from sightseeing, or for after-theatre pizza. Good fish dishes, too.
✉ Via Torino 34, 20123
☎ 02 8645 3482 🕐 Tue–Sun all day; Mon lunch only
Ⓜ Duomo

DI GENNARO €
Not far from the Duomo and good for an after-theatre meal, this pizzeria has been producing pizza classics from the old-fashioned tiled oven for many years.
✉ Via Santa Radegonda 14, 20121 ☎ 02 805 3454
🕐 Fri–Wed all day
Ⓜ Duomo

IL MOZZO €–€€
Popular with the fashionable Milanese, and away from the usual tourist spots, Il Mozzo produces some high quality cooking and tasty pizza—choose your own toppings.
✉ Via Marghera 22, 20149
☎ 02 498 4676
🕐 Thur–Tue all day
Ⓜ De Angeli, Wagner

RINO VECCHIA NAPOLI €
A little farther out but considered one of the better places in Milan for Neapolitan pizza. Reservations advised.
✉ Via Chavez 4, 20131
☎ 02 261 9056 🕐 Tue–Sat all day; Sun dinner only
Ⓜ Loreto/Udine

SAN LORENZO €
Nice venue with a garden, which is heated in winter. The San Lorenzo uses organic ingredients in their excellent pizza.
✉ Via dei Fabbri 1, 20123
☎ 02 837 2870 🕐 Daily
Ⓜ Sant'Ambrigio

TRADIZIONALE €
This busy pizzeria in the canal area, is furnished with Milanese antiques. Not just delicious pizza, but fish and pasta too. Reservations advised.
✉ Ripa di Porta Ticinese 7, 20123 ☎ 02 839 5133
🕐 Thu–Tue lunch, dinner; Wed dinner only Ⓜ Porta Genova

TRANSATLANTICO €
Well cooked pizza in this art nouveau pizzeria. Try one of the unusual combinations, such as one stuffed with mussels and squid.
✉ Via Malpighi Marcello 3, 20129 ☎ 02 2952 6098
🕐 Wed–Mon daily
Ⓜ Porta Venezia

A PLETHORA OF PIZZA
There's pizza and there's pizza. Every city in the world produces this famous Italian dish but it never tastes the same as in the country of its birth and you will find some of the best in Milan. Seek out the pizzerias where the food is cooked in the traditional manner in wood-fired ovens (forno a legna). They are usually thin crust and made to age-old recipes, and the best ones are normally prepared by one of the many Neapolitan chefs working in the city. A true Italian pizza does not include exotic toppings such as pineapple or sweetcorn.

Cafés, Bars & Gelaterie

ANYONE FOR COFFEE?

Coffee in Milan is not a simple affair. The Milanese have coffees to suit different types of food or to be drunk at different times of day. Cappuccino, or the longer and milkier *caffè latte,* are often the choice at breakfast, followed by espresso for a short kick-start of caffeine later in the day. Cappuccino is never drunk by Italians after lunch or dinner. Other varieties are *caffè americano* (long and watery), *caffè freddo* (iced coffee) and *caffè macchiato* (espresso 'stained' with a dash of milk).

CAFÉS & BARS

LE BICICLETTE

In a hidden street at the corner of Conca del Naviglio, the former bicycle workshop is now a trendy restaurant and bar. Good quality Italian and international food; very popular for brunch on Sundays.

✉ Conca del Naviglio 10, 20123 ☎ 02 839 4177
🕐 Tue–Sun dinner only; Sunday brunch 🚇 Sant'Agostino, Porta Genova

BIFFI

Biffi has been around since the end of the 19th century and is the place to try their own *panettone* (▶ 18). Come here for breakfast before shopping or for an aperitif afterwards.
✉ Corso Magenta 87, 20123 ☎ 02 4800 6702 🕐 Tue–Sun
🚇 Conciliazione

BINDI

For mouth-watering cream cakes and pastries drop in at this bright and cheery local café on the corner of the piazzale opposite the Stazione Ferrovie Nord.
✉ Piazalle Cardorna 9, 20121 ☎ 02 8645 1178 🕐 Mon–Sat
🚇 Cadorna

CAFFÉ MARTINI

At this café/bar, seating is either in the upper balcony area, with mirrors and chandeliers, or outside under canopies with heaters. Good snacks such as *panini* and salads.
✉ Via di Mercanti 21, 20123 ☎ 02 7200 0366 🕐 Daily
🚇 Cordusio

COVA

In business since 1817, this is an ideal stop for a break from shopping. It is expensive but the coffee and cakes are irresistible.
✉ Via Montenapoleone 8, 20121 ☎ 02 7600 0578
🕐 Mon–Sat 🚇 San Babila, Montenapoleone

EMPORIO ARMANI CAFFÉ

Take a break for coffee, pastries, light lunches, juices or a cocktail when browsing this sleek store, the flagship of the famous designer.
✉ Via Manzoni 31, 20121
☎ 02 7231 8680
🕐 Mon–Sat
🚇 Montenapoleone

MAGENTA

A smart clientele is attracted to this lovely old café and bar with art nouveau decoration. Good snacks by day.
✉ Via Carducci, 13, 20123
☎ 02 805 3808 🕐 Tue–Sun
🚇 Cadorna

MARCHESI

Enjoy the pastries, tarts, salads and much more at this Milan institution. Take away some sweets, cakes or chocolates—the gift-wrapping is a joy.
✉ Via Santa Maria alla Porta 11a, 20123 ☎ 02 876 730
🕐 Tue–Sun 🚇 Cordusio, Cairoli

PECK

On the top floor of a superb food and wine shop. Choose from a light lunch or settle for cakes or pastries—all will satisfy and all are of a high standard.

✉ Via Spadari 9, 20123 ☎ 02 860 842 🕐 Mon–Sat 🚇 Duomo

SANT'AMBROEUS
The ultimate pastry shop that oozes class. Wonderful window displays get the taste buds going. Beautiful tearoom and tables outside.
✉ Corso Matteotti 7, 20121 ☎ 02 7600 0540 🕐 Daily, closed 3 weeks Aug 🚇 San Babila

VICTORIA CAFFÈ
Discreet café behind the Piazza della Scala; the perfect spot for a pizza or pasta lunch, an early evening drink or after dinner nightcap.
✉ Via Clerici 1, 20121 ☎ 02 805 3598/869 0792 🕐 Daily 🚇 Duomo

ZUCCA IN GALLERIA
Famous Milan bar with an outside terrace ideal for people-watching. Coffee, lunch or evening drink—the choice is yours but prepare to pay a high price.
✉ Galleria Vittorio Emanuele 12, 20121 ☎ 02 8646 4435 🕐 Tue–Sun. Closed Aug 🚇 Duomo

GELATERIA
LA BOTTEGA DEL GELATO
This *gelateria*, not far from the central station, has been in business since the mid-19th century. Delicious ice-cream, including peach, passion fruit, melon and tamarillo.
✉ Via Pergolesi 3, 20124 ☎ 02 2940 0076 🕐 Thu–Tue 🚇 Caiazzo

IL GABBIANO
Near the Duomo, this *gelateria* sells milkshakes and fruit salad as well as a large selection of ice-cream and sorbets. You can also sit outside.
✉ Via Ugo Foscolo 3, 20121 ☎ 02 7202 2411 🕐 Daily 🚇 Duomo

GELATARIA ECOLOGICA
Ice-cream made from natural ingredients, ranging from the unusual to the exotic. The whipped cream and wild strawberry is divine.
✉ Corso di Porta Ticinese 40, 20123 ☎ 02 5810 1872 🕐 Thu–Tue 🚇 Missori

ODEON
Popular *gelateria* near the Duomo with a huge selection of ice-cream, all made using fresh milk.
✉ Pizza Duomo 2, 220123 ☎ 02 8646 1669 🕐 Thu–Tue 🚇 Duomo

ORSI
This *gelateria* down by the canal wins in summer with its nice terrace. The variety of ices is impressive—blueberry and zabaglione to name just two.
✉ Via Torricelli 19, 20136 ☎ 02 8940 6807 🕐 Daily 🚇 Romolo

VIEL
Viel has been in business producing natural ice-cream since the 1940s. This is one of four branches in the city. Delicious selection of fresh fruit.
✉ Corso Garibaldi 12, 20121 ☎ 02 8691 5489 🕐 Daily 🚇 Garibaldi

ITALIAN ICE-CREAM

The Italians justifiably pride themselves on their superior ice-cream, and Milan regards itself as one of the best ice-cream making areas in the country. There are gelaterie dating back to the mid-19th century that are still in business, some have as many as 100 different varieties on offer. Many make their ice-cream with all natural ingredients and you often find a wonderful array of fresh fruits to accompany your choice.

Fashion

OPENING HOURS

As a general rule, shops in Milan are open daily from 9.30am to 1pm, when they close for lunch. They reopen in the afternoon from 3.30 to 7.30, although many in the city no longer close for lunch. Most shops are closed on Sundays and Monday mornings, but food shops tend to close Monday afternoon (except for supermarkets). Many shops close throughout most of August. Some specialist establishments differ from these opening hours, and department stores normally stay open all day, every day.

HOME-GROWN

Milan-born designer Giorgio Armani began his career as a window dresser at the city's La Rinascente department store, and in 1961 progressed to the menswear shop Nino Cerruti. In 1975, Armani branched out alone, and within 10 years had become a household name when he revolutionized the industry with his more wearable and less expensive collection. The Armani Empire took another giant leap forward in 2000, when it opened its flagship store, Emporio Armani (see right), in Milan. According to *Forbes Celebrity 100 List*, Giorgio Armani was the highest earning fashion designer in 1999 at £135 million.

10 CORSO COMO

A future shock of unisex clothes, *objets d'art* and bags. Groundbreaking styles that are not for the fainthearted.

✉ Corso Como 10, 20154
☎ 02 2900 2674 🚇 Garibaldi

ARMANI

The flagship Armani shop is a veritable fashion megastore. The 6,000sq m (21,500sq ft) of floor space pioneered designer shopping for men, women and children, with fashion, accessories, lingerie and much more all under one roof.

✉ Via Manzoni 31, 20121
☎ 02 7231 8600
🚇 Montenapoleone

B-FLY

This customized Levi's shop is a real boon for jeans aficionados. All items have been abused enough with scissors, spray cans and threads to be called one-off. The hand-crafting is reflected in the price.

✉ Corso di Porta Ticinese 46, 20123 ☎ 02 8942 3178
🚇 Sant'Ambrogio
🚋 Tram 3

BIFFI

The place to shop for classic men's and women's designer names; watch for new emerging talent.

✉ Corso Genova 6, 20123
☎ 02 831 1601
🚇 Porta Genova

CHANEL

Browse the fashion legend's latest creations at this retro boutique.

✉ Via Sant'Andrea 10/a, 20121

☎ 02 782 514 🚇 San Babila

DIESEL

Jeans fans should not miss this Diesel Experimental range flagship store where all items are customized.

✉ Corso di Porta Ticinese 44, 20123 ☎ 02 8942 0916
🚇 Sant'Ambrogio
🚋 Tram 3

FENDI

From recent beginnings (in high-fashion furs), the Fendi sisters have built a powerful fashion, perfume and accessories empire. Clothes are classic, sleek and stylish.

✉ Via Sant'Andrea 16, 20121
☎ 02 799 544 🚇 San Babila

GUCCI

Fitted out with elegant, sharp lines in wood and steel, this shop is central to the Gucci Empire.

✉ Via Pietro Verri 10, 20121
☎ 02 771 271 🚇 San Babila

GUESS

There's a huge choice for men and women at this New York designer's megastore.

✉ Piazza San Bibila 4b, 20122
☎ 02 7639 2070 🚇 San Babila

JIL SANDER

Avant-garde cuts and attention to detail are the trademarks of this famous German designer. Styles for both men and women.

✉ Via Pietro Verri 6, 20121
☎ 02 777 2991 🚇 San Babila

KRIZIA

Flies lower in the international fashion firmament than the likes of Armani and Versace,

but has a high profile in Italy, especially for knitwear.
✉ Via della Spiga 23, 20121
☎ 02 7600 8429 Ⓜ San Babila

LA PERLA
Sultry and sophisticated underwear and swimwear made in the finest fabrics.
✉ Via Montenapoleone 2, 20121 ☎ 02 7600 0460
Ⓜ San Babila

LAURA BIAGIOTTI
Easy to wear fashion, gentle on the eye and less aggressively 'high fashion' than some other designers.
✉ Via Borgospesso 19, 20121
☎ 02 799 659
Ⓜ Montenapoleone

MAX MARA
A popular mid-range label known for suits, separates, knitwear and accessories at fair prices.
✉ Corso Vittorio Emanuele II (corner of Galleria de Cristoforis), 20122 ☎ 02 7600 8849
Ⓜ San Bibila

MIU MIU
Urban chic from the House of Prada, with creations such as plastic trousers, steel-striped skirts and shiny T-shirts. Check out the high-tech interior.
✉ Corso Venezia 3, 20121
☎ 02 7601 4448 Ⓜ San Babila

PURPLE
Expensive youth fashion including T-shirt designs, many from the Fake brand, hog the limelight in the store's glass front.

✉ Corso di Porta Ticinese 22, 20123 ☎ 02 8942 4476
Ⓜ Sant'Ambrogio 🚋 Tram 3

PRADA
The outside of this flagship branch of Prada has graced a thousand fashion photographs, and the window display is second to none.
✉ Galleria Vittorio Emanuele II 63, 20122 ☎ 02 876 979
Ⓜ San Babila

ROBERTO CAVALLI
You can feel the elegance as you enter this chic boutique owned by Italian fashion mogul Roberto Cavalli. Animal skin designs are commonplace.
✉ Via della Spiga 42, 20121
☎ 02 7602 0900
Ⓜ Montenapoleone

SISLEY
This Italian designer's huge window displays draw the shoppers in droves. Quality Italian men's shirts, ladies' T-shirts and the latest lingerie.
✉ Via Dogana 4, 20123 ☎ 02 8050 9415 Ⓜ Duomo

VERSACE
Versace's trademark bright, bold colour combinations that need plenty of panache and cash to carry them off.
✉ Via Montenapoleone, 20121
☎ 02 7600 8528 Ⓜ San Babila

YVES SAINT LAURENT
Classic styles for men and women, but with a slightly different slant.
✉ Via Pietro Verri 8, 20121
☎ 02 7600 0573 Ⓜ San Babila

FASHION SHOWS

Milan was first catapulted into the limelight as Europe's fashion capital in 1971, when Italy's largest international fashion show (held in Florence since 1951) was moved here. Today, the autumn and winter collections of Italy's leading designers such as Versace and Dolce & Gabbana, grace the catwalks at the Fiera di Milano in early March. The spring and summer collections take the stage in September. Throughout the duration of these dazzling shows, Milan is alive with top designers, models and celebrities.

Leather Goods & Shoes

WORKING WITH WASTE

Riedizioni is the trademark of a series of products made from industrial waste. The textile industry creates lots of waste and Italian designer Luisa Cevese came up with this innovative material by combining recyled textile scraps with plastic. Her range of products, from bags and wallets to cushions and place mats, uses various types of textile waste and plastic, with different properties producing individual results. If you would like to buy one of these unique, but very expensive, products visit the Riedizione shop. ✉ Via San Maurilio 3, 20123 ☎ 02 801 088

BRUNO MAGLI
A middle to up-scale chain selling incredibly elegant, classic Italian shoes.
✉ Corso Vittorio Emanuele II (corner of Via San Paolo), 20122 ☎ 02 865 695
Ⓜ San Babila

FAUSTO SANTINI
Fausto Santini's innovative and occasionally bizarre shoes are aimed at the young and daring. Wear them if you dare!
✉ Via Montenapoleone 1, 20121 ☎ 02 7600 1958
Ⓜ San Babila

FERRAGAMO SALVATORE
Italy's most famous shoe designer, whose stores grace exclusive shopping streets all over the world, also has a branch here in Milan.
✉ Via Montenapoleone 3, 20121 ☎ 02 7600 0054
Ⓜ San Babila

FRATELLI ROSSETTI
This family company, founded 30 years ago by the brothers Renzo and Renato, pushes Ferragamo (see above) hard for the title of Italy's best shoe store. Classic and current styles at slightly lower prices than its rival.
✉ Via Montenapoleone 1, 20121 ☎ 02 7602 1650
Ⓜ San Babila

FURLA
Chic leather bags and belts in high-fashion, minimalist designs, but with an original twist. Also scarves and shoes. Affordable prices.
✉ Corso Vittorio Emanuele II (corner of Piazza Liberty), 20122 ☎ 02 796 943
Ⓜ San Babila

LE SILLA
A must for lovers of expensive shoes. Women's footwear, from the smart to the seductive and scandalous, all displayed in an ultra-modern store.
✉ Corso Venezia 9, 20121 ☎ 02 7600 5286
Ⓜ San Babila

LOUIS VUITTON
Get your hands on the world's most distinctive luggage at the Milan branch of this well-known store. Branded bags, purses and cases for the international jet set.
✉ Via Montenapoleone 2, 20121 ☎ 02 777 1711
Ⓜ San Babila

MANDARINA DUCK
On two floors, one of Italy's leading luggage stores, trading on a stunning blend of style and function.
✉ Via Orefici 10, 20123 ☎ 02 8646 2198
Ⓜ Cordusio

POLLINI
Up-to-the minute boots and bags for men and women in lively styles.
✉ Corso Vittorio Emanuele II 30, 20122 ☎ 02 794 912
Ⓜ San Babila

SERMONETA
Handmade leather gloves in every size, shade and style you can imagine.
✉ Via della Spiga 46, 20121 ☎ 02 7631 8303
Ⓜ San Babila

Accessories

ACQUA DI PARMA
Items to pamper the feet, body, face and scalp, and leather pouches in which to put your new purchases.
✉ 3 Via Gesù, 20121
☎ 02 7602 3307
Ⓜ Montenapoleone

ALAN JOURNO
Crazy bags, hats and lots more in eccentric styles displayed around a stainless steel and glass staircase that spirals over three levels.
✉ Via della Spiga 36, 20121
☎ 02 7600 1309
Ⓜ Montenapoleone

ANDREW'S TIES
Italian ties made of wool, silk and cashmere in every imaginable shade and design. Shirts and sweaters as well.
✉ Galleria Vittorio Emanuele II, 20121 ☎ 02 860 935
Ⓜ Duomo

BORSALINO
Milan's oldest milliners should be the first port of call if you are looking to buy a hat.
✉ Galleria Vittorio Emanuele II, 20121 ☎ 02 8901 5436
Ⓜ Duomo

BULGARI
The Milan branch of the world-famous fashion jeweller and watch-maker.
✉ Via della Spiga 6, 20121
☎ 02 777 001
Ⓜ San Babila

CARTIER
Police-guarded Cartier's has gold, silver and porcelain that is the stuff of dreams, as are the prices.
✉ Via Montenapoleone 21, 20121 ☎ 02 7600 1610
Ⓜ San Babila

DAMIANI
Founded in Milan in 1924, this jeweller's dramatic marble façade is as sparkling as the bold original designs inside.
✉ Via Montenapoleone 16, 20121 ☎ 02 7602 8088
Ⓜ San Babila

DIEGO DELLA PALMA
Lipsticks, powders and paints from this household name among Italy's make-up elite. Knowledgeable staff can advise you on the products to use to suit your skin tone.
✉ 15 Via Madonnina, 20121
☎ 02 876 818
Ⓜ Lanza

OTTICA DEL CORSO
Beautiful Italian eyewear including designer ranges from Anna Sui and Gucci. Prices are somewhat cheaper than similar products in the Galleria Vittorio Emanuele. Also sexy, 1970s-style sunglasses.
✉ 58 Corso di Porta Ticinese, 20123 ☎ 02 5810 1525
Ⓜ Sant'Ambrogio
🚊 Tram 3

TIFFANY & CO
Legendary jewellers selling highly desirable crystals, gold and silverware, clocks and jewellery, but at prices that suit only the extremely rich.
✉ Via della Spiga 19a, 20121
☎ 02 7602 2321
Ⓜ San Babila

WHERE DID YOU GET THAT HAT?
Although women from an early stage were expected to cover their heads, it was not until the 17th century that women's headgear began to emerge in its own right. The word 'milliner'–a maker of women's hats–was first recorded in 1529, and then referred to the products for which Milan was Europe's leading manufacturer–ribbons and gloves. The Milanese haberdashers who imported such fineries were called 'Millaners' from which the word was eventually derived.

Art & Antiques

IS IT ANTIQUE?

When searching for that special piece, bear in mind that under Italian law an antique need only be made of old materials. For this reason, what would be called reproduction elsewhere is quite legally called an antique in Italy. Hundreds of shops all over Milan sell so-called antiques, but the narrow, cobbled lanes of the Brera district and the canal area are particularly pleasant places to browse.

ANTICHITÀ CAIATI

This exclusive gallery specializes in Venetian landscapes and 17th- and 18th-century Italian paintings.
✉ Via Gesú 17, 20121
☎ 02 794 866
Ⓜ Montenapoleone

CARLO ORSI

The fine paintings, bronze sculpture, furniture and precious stones on sale here are a collector's dream.
✉ Via Bagutta 14, 20121
☎ 02 7600 2214
Ⓜ San Babila

FRANCO SABATELLI

Exclusive picture framer of international repute who sells and restores frames dating from the 16th century.
✉ Via Fiori Chiari 5, 20121
☎ 02 805 2688
Ⓜ Lanza

IL BAZAR DEL NAVIGLIO GRANDE

Signor Franzini's collection of pre-WWII toys would delight any child (and adult): porcelain dolls, toy trains, marionettes, rocking horses, teddy bears and much more.
✉ Ripa di Porta Ticinese 27, 20123 ☎ 02 832 2103
Ⓜ Porta Genova

L'ANTICA FONTE

An elegant shop specializing in antique furniture, where the owner is more than willing to show off his Louis XVI and early 19th-century pieces.
✉ Via San Damiano 5, 20122
🕐 02 7600 0236
Ⓜ San Babila

MERCATO D'ANTIQUARIATO DI BRERA

Enthusiasts should not miss this monthly antiques market of about 70 stalls laden with collectables at bargain prices.
✉ Via Fiori Chiari, 20121
🕐 8.30–6 third Sun of month
Ⓜ Lanza

MERCATONE DEL NAVIGLIO GRANDE

This extensive canalside market selling antique objects and bric-à-brac is the best in the city.
✉ Alzaia Naviglio Grande, 20144 🕐 Last Sun of month
Ⓜ Porta Genova

OLD ENGLISH FURNITURE

If you like 18th- and 19th-century English furniture, head for this shop, which has many examples on display.
✉ Piazza San Simpliciano 6, 20121 ☎ 02 877 807
Ⓜ Lanza

PONTREMOLI

Beautifully displayed porcelain and glass, from the 18th century to art nouveau, plus Louis XV and XVI furniture, and European and Italian paintings.
✉ Via Montenapoleone 22, 20121 ☎ 02 7600 1394
Ⓜ San Babila

PORTOBELLO

A wealth of items such as Lalique and Murano glass, art nouveau objects and china animals.
✉ Corso Magenta 11, 20123
☎ 02 874 709
Ⓜ Cadorna

Home Design & Furnishing

ALESSI
Alessi has everything for the home and office. Drinks accessories, from wine coolers to corkscrews, and a myriad of containers, textiles, trays and items for children's rooms.
✉ Corso Matteotti 9, 20121
☎ 02 795 726
🚇 San Babila

ARTEMIDE
Renowned for forthright modern designs created by top designers, the products are displayed to best effect in a gallery-like showroom.
✉ Corso Monforte 19, 20122
☎ 02 7600 6930
🚇 San Babila

DA DRIADE
Founded in 1968, Da Driade is always seeking new trends, many of which go on to be collectors' items. The products are showcased in beautiful display rooms.
✉ Via Manzoni 30, 20121
☎ 02 7602 3098
🚇 Montenapoleone

DE PADOVA
Elegance and simplicity of design are key at this shop for the discerning homeowner. Only the finest materials are used.
✉ Corso Venezia 14, 20121
☎ 02 777 201 🚇 San Babila, Palestro

KARTELL
Minimal moulded furnishings: bowls, cups, seats and lamp stands made almost entirely from bright and stunningly curved plastic.
✉ Via Turati 11, 20122 ☎ 02 659 7916 🚇 Turati

FLOS
High quality ultra-modern lighting for the home and office, including contemporary creations by famous names, such as Phillippe Starck and Jasper Morrison.
✉ Corso Monforte 9, 20122
☎ 02 7600 3639
🚇 San Babila

HIGH-TECH
Packed to the gunnels with every conceivable item for the design-conscious homeowner, from housewares and bathroom accessories to office equipment and garden furniture and everything in between.
✉ Piazza XXV Aprile 12, 20124
☎ 02 624 1101 🚇 Moscova, Garibaldi

MIRABELLO
The trade name Mirabello is a symbol of high quality and youthful design. The fun, fresh ideas encompass household linens, curtains, fabrics and more.
✉ Via Montebello (corner of Via San Marco), 20121
☎ 02 654 887 🚇 Turati, Moscova

VETRERIE DI EMPOLI SPA
Gorgeous hand-decorated glasses, chandeliers, vases and fruit dishes: this shop is a must for glass collectors.
✉ Via Montenapoleone 14, 20121 ☎ 02 7600 8791
🚇 Montenapoleone

DEPARTMENT STORES
Department stores are still rather alien to most Italians and Milan only has a handful. The best department store is La Rinascente (✉ Via Radegonda 3 ☎ 02 88 521), a monumental shop opposite the Duomo. It stretches over six floors, and sells almost everything you could possibly want. Coin (✉ Piazza Cinque Giornate 1/a ☎ 02 5519 2083) is also good, and sells a full range of quality products. More downmarket, Upim Duomo (✉ Via Torino/Via Spadari ☎ 02 8901 0750) sells most items at really low prices.

77

Food & Wine

ITALIAN CAKES

There are three main types of Italian cake. *Brioche* (pastries) are made with sweet yeast dough and often filled with a delicious, oozing custard. *Torte* (cakes) tend to be tarts, such as the ubiquitous *torta della nanna* (granny's cake), a kind of cake in tart form, or *torta di ricotta*, in which ricotta is mixed with sugar and candied peel. Then there are all kinds of little cookies, most of which contain nuts and have names such as the accurately named *brutti ma buoni* (ugly but good).

ARMANDOLA

An elegant deli that reflects its exclusive location in its prices. But the tempting aroma of cheese and the display of freshly made pastas and jars of truffles make it worth every penny.
✉ Via della Spiga 50, 20121
☎ 02 7602 1657
🚇 Montenapoleone

BAITA DEL FORMAGGIO

Quality Italian, and some French, cheese at good prices. As it is vacuum-packed for freshness, it makes an ideal gift to take home.
✉ Via Paolo Sarpi 31, 20121
☎ 02 331 9651 🚇 Moscova

DROGHERIA PARINI

Upstairs for mouth-watering confectionery and downstairs to the arched cellar for wines and spirits, cookies, organic jams and jellies, compotes and chutneys, and excellent blends of coffee and tea—all beautifully gift-wrapped.
✉ Via Borgospesso 1, 20121
☎ 02 7600 2303
🚇 Montenapoleone

LA FUNGHERIA

Quality mushrooms and truffles from a shop whose name is known in Milan for mushroom production by organic methods.
✉ Via Marghera 14, 20149
☎ 02 439 0089 🚇 Wagner, De Angeli

GARBAGNATI

The most famous bakery in Milan, especially renowned for its *panettone*.
✉ Via Victor Hugo 3, 20123
☎ 02 860 905 🚇 Duomo

GIOVANNI GALLI

The shop for those who love all things sweet. The marrons glacés are legendary, and the traditional sweets, biscuits and pralines are pretty good, too.
✉ Corso di Porta Romana 2, 20122 ☎ 02 8645 3112
🚇 Missori

N'OMBRA DE VIN

This shop has a fine collection of wines from Italy, France and the New World. Tastings
✉ Via San Marco 2, 20121
☎ 02 659 9650 🚇 Turati, Moscova

PASTICCERIA MARCHESI

Popular with the Milanese and little changed in appearance since 1824. Sample the chocolates, pralines and delicate cakes. Tastings
✉ Via Santa Maria alla Porta 11/a, 20123 ☎ 02 876 730
🚇 Cairoli

PECK

Probably Milan's most prestigious delicatessen, with numerous different stalls specializing in bread, cheese, seafood, salami, marinated vegetables and other Mediterranean delights.
✉ Via Spadari 9, 20121 ☎ 02 875 358 🚇 Duomo

RANIERI

One of Milan's great *patisserie* institutions. The pineapple *panettone* is particularly good.
✉ Via della Moscova 7, 20121
☎ 02 659 5308 🚇 Turati

Books, Music & Stationery

BUSCEMI DISCHI
One of the city's oldest and most famous record stores, split between two shops. Don't hesitate to ask for assistance if you can't find what you want on the crammed shelves.
✉ Corso Magenta 31, 20123
☎ 02 804 103
🚇 Cadorna

CARTOLERIA RUFFINI
See the craftsman at work out the back producing handmade notebooks, albums, boxes and letter racks, which are then sold at the front of this traditional old shop.
✉ Via Ruffini 1, 20123
☎ 02 463 074
🚇 Conciliazione

DISCOVERY
Browse through rare vinyl albums by the Beatles, Lou Reed and Jimi Hendrix, all priced around €8. Picture discs cost slightly more.
✉ Passaggio Santa Margherita (just off Piazza Mercanti), 20123
☎ 02 7202 2893
🚇 Duomo

ENGLISH BOOKSHOP
The most varied selection of English-language fiction and non-fiction books in Milan; also videos, audio books and a large kids' section.
✉ Via Mascheroni 12, 20145
☎ 02 469 4468
🚇 Conciliazione

FELTRINELLI INTERNATIONAL
This branch of the well-known bookstore is where the world's fashion hierarchy come to buy their English and American *Vogues*, *Elles* and *Cosmopolitans*.
✉ Piazza Cavour 2, 20122
☎ 02 659 5644 🚇 Turati

LIBRERIA HOEPLI
Established in 1870, this bookshop, extending over six floors, has the most extensive stock in Milan of books in any language, on any subject.
✉ Via Hoepli 5, 20121
☎ 02 864 871
🚇 Duomo

MASTRI CARTAI EDITORI
Refined handmade paper in unconventional shades and designs is used to produce innovative items such as lampholders, picture frames and boxes.
✉ Corso Garibaldi 26/34, 20121 ☎ 02 8052 3111
🚇 Lanza

PAPIER
A delightful stationers selling handcrafted items made from natural, undyed paper and paper produced using coconut, cotton and silk.
✉ Via San Maurillo 4, 20123
☎ 02 865 221 🚇 Duomo, Cordusio

RICORDI MEGASTORE
One of Italy's best music stores and the first of its kind in Milan, selling books on composers and their works, recorded music and sheet music, plus instruments. Also concert tickets available.
✉ Galleria Vittorio Emanuele II, 20121 ☎ 02 8646 0272
🚇 Duomo

MARKETS

Milan's street markets are noisy and fun, selling anything from cheeses and salamis to clothes and second-hand books, plus there are good specialist markets as well. Markets fill the waterfronts around the canals, notably Mercato del Sabato on Viale Papiniano, which offers great designer-label bargains in clothes, shoes and bags, and there is a flea market (Fiera di Sinigaglia) at Viale Gabriele d'Annunzio on Saturday. A huge antique market stretches alongside the canals on the last Sunday of each month. Elsewhere in the city other good general markets are at Via San Marco on Thursday morning, Via Zuretti on Wednesday morning and Via Crema on Friday morning.

Theatre & Cinema

THEATRES

TEATRO ARSENALE

The place to come for searing comedy, cutting-edge dramas and groundbreaking acting by up-and-coming thespians. Tickets are available from the venue itself, near Via Torino, daily from 1pm. Most performances are in Italian only.
www.teatroarsenale.org ✉ Via Correnti 11, 20122 ☎ 02 8321 1999, information 02 837 5896 🚇 Sant'Ambrogio

TEATRO CARCANO

First opened to the public in 1803, the theatre underwent substantial changes in the 1980s. Theatrical productions include staged versions of films, and it is also used for lectures by the university.
www.teatrocarcano.com ✉ Corso di Porta Romana 63, 20122 ☎ 02 5518 1362/5518 1377 🚇 Crocetta

TEATRO CIAK

A popular venue for a variety of performance styles, including comedy, cabaret and murder mystery plays. A great place to spot emerging talent. Reserve in advance.
www.teatrociak.com ✉ Via Sangallo 33, 20133 ☎ 02 7611 0093 🚇 Dateo 🚋 Tram 5

TEATRO FILODRAMMATICI

Mainly Italian-language performances emerge from this politically left-leaning playhouse, but

there are many non-political plays including some excellent black comedies and musicals. Easy to find, opposite La Scala.
www.teatrofilodrammatici.it ✉ Piazza della Scala 1, 20121 ☎ 02 869 3659 🚇 Montenapoleone

TEATRO LITTA

Children's plays make up the lion's share of performances here. The magic and dance displays will delight English-speaking kids, although the Italian language drama shows may be beyond them. A peek inside the classic baroque theatre is worth it for those interested in architecture.
www.teatrolitta.it ✉ Corso Magenta 24, 20123 ☎ 02 8645 4545; 🚇 Cadorna

TEATRO MANZONI

This theatre is particularly popular with the Milanese and produces a variety of performances, including serious drama such as plays by Chekhov and Brecht, Italian plays, one-man shows, stand-up comedy, classical music concerts and musicals; Sunday mornings for jazz.
www.teatromanzoni.it ✉ Via Alessandro Manzoni 42, 20121 ☎ 02 763 6901 🚇 Montenapoleone

TEATRO NUOVO

All types of theatre are staged here including some excellent comedy, musicals and dance productions. There is

TICKET INFORMATION

Tickets for theatre and concerts can booked through agencies and also from specialist booking offices such as the Ricordi Box Office in Galleria Vittorio Emanuele II (☎ 02 869 0683), in the Virgin Megastore in Piazza Duomo (☎ 02 7209 8657) and in the Stazione Centrale (☎ 02 669 6757). Tickets for La Scala need to be purchased well in advance—it may be possible on very rare occasions to get a ticket two hours before a performance.

capacity for over 1,000 people, who come to see performances by some of the famous actors who appear here regularly.
www.teatronouvo.it
✉ Piazza San Babila, 20121
☎ 02 7600 0086 Ⓜ San Babila

TEATRO SAN BABILA

Tradition is the key here, and the Milanese flock to see famous actors and directors stage their best-loved works of drama in this 500-seat theatre. Reserve well in advance.
✉ Corso Venezia 2/a, 20121
☎ 02 7600 2985 Ⓜ San Babila

TEATRO SMERALDO

Smeraldo is particularly popular for its musicals such as *Chicago*, which played in 2004, and *Jesus Christ Superstar* in 2003. The theatre seats over 2,000 people and is also a venue for dance, drama and concerts.
✉ Piazza XXV Aprile 10, 20154
☎ 02 2900 6767 Ⓜ Moscova, Garibaldi

CINEMAS

ANTEO

One of Milan's leading original language cinemas, with a slant on art house rather than mainstream pictures. Films from countries such as Sweden, Japan or France are often shown with English subtitles.
www.anteospaziocinema.com
✉ Via Milazzo 9, 20121 ☎ 02 659 7732 Ⓜ Moscova

COLESSEO

There is a choice of three screens, called the Visconti, Allen and Chaplin—all names with movie connections—plus a bar.
✉ Viale Monte Nero 84, 20135
☎ 02 5990 1361 Ⓜ Porta Romano

DUCALE

The Ducale has been converted from an old cinema into a modern four-screen movie house with a pleasant bar.
✉ Piazza Napoli 27, 20146
☎ 02 4771 9279 Ⓜ Porta Genova

GLORIA

This renovated cinema comprises two theatres, the Garbo and the Marilyn. Big screens and a good sound system. Bar.
✉ Corso Vercelli 18, 20144
☎ 02 4800 8908 Ⓜ Pagano, Conciliazione

ODEON

A huge mainstream cinema in the middle of Milan showing the latest American blockbusters, many in their original language, so you can still catch the latest releases from home. This ten-screen complex has good access for visitors with disabilities.
✉ Via Santa Radegonda 8, 20121 ☎ 02 874 547 Ⓜ Duomo

PLINIUS

Six screens showing the latest mainstream films.
✉ Viale Abruzzi 28–30, 20131
☎ 02 2953 1103 Ⓜ Loreto, Lima

THE BIG SCREEN

Going to the cinema is a popular pastime for the Milanese and there are a number of cinemas close to the heart of the city. There are also many multiplexes further out: Arcadia (☎ 02 9541 6444), 28km (18 miles) east of the city at Melzo, is part of a huge site with shops and restaurants, and houses Energia, the biggest screen in Italy.

Live Music Venues

CLASSICAL & DANCE

AUDITORIUM DI MILANO

A multi-purpose hall and the home of the Orchestra Sinfonica di Milano Guiseppe Verdi. Symphony concerts, choral works and chamber music; also jazz and light music.

✉ Via Torricelli, corner Corso S. Gottardo, 20136 ☎ 02 8338 9201/2/3 🚇 Romolo, then trolley bus 90, 91 🚌 59

CRT TEATRO DELL'ARTE

Most performances are in Italian but the passionate music and contemporary dance displays will need no translation. Several yearly dance festivals with top directors, dancers and actors.

www.teatrocrt.org
✉ Viale Alemagna 6, 20121 ☎ 02 8901 1644 🚇 Cadorna

TEATRO ALLA SCALA

Opera, classical and the occasional musical boom out from Milan's, and possibly the world's, most prestigious playhouse. It's not just famous names at La Scala; Maria Callas was unknown when she made her debut here. The venue has a bar, museum, visitor centre and an excellent bookshop with many titles in English.

www.teatroallascala.org
✉ Piazza della Scala, 20121 ☎ 02 7200 3744 🚇 Montenapoleone

TUNNEL

An unusual and unique space created in a converted warehouse under the central station. A variety of live music, DJ evenings, poetry readings, film shows and exhibitions, and you can enjoy cocktails at the bar. Prices are lower than other more conventional venues in the city.

✉ Via Samartini 30, 20125 ☎ 02 6671 1370 🚇 Centrale FS

CONTEMPORARY

BLUE NOTE

Perfect venue for listening to top quality international jazz.

✉ Via Borsieri 37, 20159 ☎ 02 690 1688 🚇 Garibaldi

GRILLOPARLANTE

Famous musicians as well as up and coming bands perform here. Jazz, blues, rock and country with occasional classical music, too.

✉ Alzaia Naviglio Grande 36, 20144 ☎ 02 8940 9321 🚇 Porta Genova

SAKALIN

Rock, punk and heavy metal, with a warm welcome extended to all visiting rock fans.

✉ Via Pezzotti 52, 20141 ☎ 02 8950 3509 🚇 Wagner

SCIMMIE

A fantastic, happening venue for jazz, blues and Brazilian beats. Feast on great value pizza and snacks as you watch the shows.

www.scimmie.it
✉ Via Ascanio Sforza 49, 20122 ☎ 02 8940 2874 🚇 Porta Genova

TRANSILVANIA

There is more of a youthful feel than most rock clubs at this extremely noisy venue, a hot spot for visiting rockers. Details of live bands are on the website.

www.transilvanialive.it
✉ Via Paravia 59, 20148 ☎ 02 4009 5472; 🚇 Bande Nere, then bus 95

Clubs & Discos

ALCATRAZ
Rock-orientated live music and disco venue frequented by the occasional famous face.
✉ Via Valtellina 25, 20121
☎ 02 6901 6352 🚇 Garibaldi

COLONY
Disco bar and restaurant on two floors with live music on Monday and cocktails on Sunday.
✉ Piazza XXIV Maggio 8, 20123 ☎ 02 5810 2766
🚇 Garibaldi

HOLLYWOOD
Getting in is neither cheap nor easy—you'll need lots of cash and your latest Galleria Emanuele outfit. But once inside you could be rubbing shoulders with Milan's beautiful people.
✉ Corso Como 15, 20154
☎ 02 655 5318 🚇 Garibaldi

LA BANQUE
A popular nightspot in a former bank, usually frequented by the after-theatre crowd. A range of music fills the dance floor, which was once the bank's vault.
✉ Via E. Porrone 6, 20121
☎ 02 8699 6565 🚇 Cordusio

MAGAZZINI GENERALI
A mixed crowd work up a sweat to a good mix of music at this nightclub, spread over two floors.
✉ Via Pietrasanta 14, 20141 ☎ 02 5521 1313
🚇 Lodi Tibb

OLD FASHION CAFÉ
Exclusive nightspot in a former ballroom that attracts a chic crowd to its theme nights. Garden in summer.

✉ Viale E. Alemagna 6, 20121
☎ 02 805 6231 🚇 Cadorna

PLASTIC
This buzzing disco for gay and straight revellers has a drag night on Tuesday. After 30 years, it's still a popular venue; not open every night, so call ahead to check.
✉ Viale Umbria 120, 20123
☎ 02 733 996 🚇 Duomo

ROLLING STONE
Listen to live rock, punk, indie and jazz at this relaxed hangout. No dress code.
✉ Corso XXII Marzo 32, 20135
☎ 02 733172
🚇 Porta Vittorio

SHOCKING
Dancing until dawn. Reputable live bands take turns with big name club DJs.
✉ Bastione di Porta Nuove 2, 20121 ☎ 02 659 5407
🚇 Garibaldi

TOCQUEVILLE
Celebrity spotting is top of the bill at ultra-cool Toqueville's Thursday and Sunday night parties. Feast on tapas all night.
✉ Via de Tocquevile 13, 20154
☎ 02 2900 2973
🚇 Garibaldi

TROPICANA CLUB LATINO
The place to go for Latin-American dancing. A mostly over-thirties crowd move to the rhythm of salsa, mambo and tango on three floors.
✉ Viale Bligny 52, 20136
☎ 02 5843 6525
🚇 Romana

DANCING TRENDS

Milan is the place to be if you are on the lookout for new music and dance trends. The city boasts hoards of discos and clubs that offer all types of music but the trend tends to lean towards a select few. Apart from the rare exceptions, clubs and discos change their name and style on a regular basis. A club that is in vogue one week can be passé the next. Entrance fees vary a lot—a system known as 'drinkcard', where you pay for your drinks at the door, is often used. Some places are free to get in but you will pay, probably over the top, for drinks.

Pubs & Bars

MILANESE BARS

From the chic and trendy to the more traditional, Milanese bars are sprinkled throughout the city, and most are open all day until 2 or 3am. They serve a vast selection of beers, wines, aperitifs, cocktails and non-alcoholic drinks, and most have a selection of snacks—some double as cafés. Many of Milan's bars have introduced an early evening 'happy hour' when drinks are cheaper. If you sit down for waiter service you will pay a premium, whether inside or out. The procedure when standing up is to pay for what you want at the cash desk, then take your receipt to the bar and repeat your order.

ATM

This curious bar attracts an up-for-it set of classy drinkers. Most of the clientele prefer dancing until the early hours to drinking.
✉ Bastione di Volta 15, 20121
☎ 02 6552 2365
🚇 Lanza

DIANA MAJESTIC BAR

Partake of sophisticated cocktails and aperitifs in the bar at the Diana Majestic Hotel (➤ 86). Sit out in the elegant gardens during summer, while the lavish lounge and opulent bar are a great pit stop in the cooler months.
✉ Viale Piave 42, 20129
☎ 02 20581
🚇 Porta Venezia

JAMAICA

Since 1920, Brera's painters and artists have flocked to this legendary haunt, and it's still popular today. The cocktails and huge salads are good.
✉ Via Brera 32, 20121
☎ 02 876 723
🚇 Montenapoleone

L'ELEPHANTE

One of the city's leading hangouts for dressed-up revellers and trendy students. Decked out with innovative plastic furniture.
✉ Via Melzo 22, 20129
☎ 02 2951 8768
🚇 Porta Venezia

MAGENTA

Friendly staff, wooden tables and a top shelf stacked full of the world's finest spirits. Every type of music from jazz to rock and punk is played on the bar's stereo system.
✉ Via Carducci 13, 20123
☎ 02 8053 3808
🚇 Cordusio

POGUE MAHONE

Those that require a night in Anglo-Saxon company, drinking Guinness and watching soccer should head for this popular Irish pub. Occasional live bands.
✉ Via Salmini 1, 20135
☎ 02 5830 9726
🚇 Porta Romana

THAT'S AMORE

One of Milan's most respected bars, attracting fashionable drinkers of all ages. Early aperitifs may descend into dance floor revelry before the night is over.
✉ Viale Monte Santo 8, 20124
☎ 02 2906 0626
🚇 Repubblica

TRATTOIR

Popular arts bar with occasional live jazz, rock or blues. Help yourself to the tasty snacks that are left on top of the bar, or sit back and soak up the cheerful atmosphere.
✉ Corso Garibaldi 1, 20121
☎ 02 801 002
🚇 Garibaldi

RED LION

A traditional English-style pub with dark wood, tartan upholstery, darts and excellent refined beer.
✉ Via Edmondo De Amicis 33, 20123 ☎ 02 5810 7444
🚇 Sant'Ambrogio

Sport

SPECTATOR SPORTS

SOCCER
AC MILAN AND INTER
Catch one of Italy's most illustrious soccer clubs, AC Milan or Inter, at the San Siro stadium on alternate weekends during the season. Tickets for matches sell out fast, so buy in advance from the clubs' shop in Via Turati, from FNAC in Via Torino, on the website or through TicketOne.
www.acmilan.com or www.inter.it
✉ Via Piccolomini 5, 20151
☎ 02 4009 2175
⏰ Sep–Jun 🚌 Lotto then free bus before matches
🚊 Tram 16

HORSE-RACING
IPPODROME DEL GALOPPO/TROTTING
For horse racing fans there is a full calendar of flat racing events from March to November. In the separate arena across the road, trotting races take place throughout the year (not August).
www.trenno.it
✉ Piazzale dello Sport, San Siro 20151 ☎ 02 482 161 🚇 Lotto
🚊 Tram 16

MOTOR RACING
ITALIAN GRAND PRIX
The Italian Grand Prix at Monza ranks alongside Monte Carlo as one of the glitziest Grands Prix on the Formula 1 circuit. Plenty of stars and models watch the race under a sea of red Ferrari flags. Ticket information can be found on the website.

www.monzanet.it
✉ Parco di Monza, 20052 Monza ☎ 039 248 2212
⏰ Sep 🚆 from Stazione Centrale

PARTICIPATORY SPORTS

TENNIS
CENTRO SPORTIVO MARIO SAINI
This tennis facility has an open-air clay court and 12 indoor synthetic courts. Equipment is available to rent. Non member welcome, but tennis whites are appreciated.
✉ Via Corelli 136, 20134
☎ 02 756 1280 ⏰ Daily dawn–dusk 🚌 38

GOLF
GOLF CLUB MILANO
This prestigious 18-hole golf course 30 minutes from Milan is close to the town of Monza. Pro shop, driving range, pool and restaurant.
www.golfclubmilano.it
✉ Viale Mulini San Giorgio 7, 20052 Monza
☎ 039 303 081

LE ROVEDINE
Milan's only public golf course lies 6km (4 miles) outside the city. Restaurant.
www.rovedine.com
✉ Via Karl Marx 18, Noverasco di Opera, 20090
☎ 02 5760 6420

SWIMMING
PISCINA SOLARI
Take a dip in this glass-covered 5-lane pool, overlooking Parco Solari.
✉ Via Montevideo 11, 20144
☎ 02 4695 278
⏰ Times vary, so phone first
🚇 Sant'Agostino

BUILDING MEZZA STADIUM
Renamed after Giuseppe Mezza in 1980, one of Italy's all-time great soccer players, this famous stadium is more commonly called San Siro, after the district surrounding it. A remarkable design: the building gives the impression that it is wrapped up by the spiralling access flights. It was originally built in 1926 as a gift from Piero Pirelli, the then president of AC Milan, and could only seat 10,000. A second tier was added in 1955 and a third plus a fibreglass roof supported by 12 cylindrical concrete towers was added in 1987, making the stadium's capacity over 85,000. The 1990 World Cup was staged at San Siro.

Luxury Hotels

Average price for a double
room per night:
Budget under €160
Mid-Range €160–350
Luxury over €350

HOTEL GRADING

Italian hotels, including those
in Milan, are classified by the
state system into five
categories, from one to five
stars. As this is based entirely
on facilities offered, it could
mean a charmingly furnished
atmospheric 2-star *pensione*
may cost less than a run-down
3-star business hotel. This is
further complicated by a
fewer-stars-less-tax situation
with some hoteliers happy not
to upgrade themselves.

FOUR SEASONS

A beautifully restored
15th-century monastery
in the Quad d'Oro set
around a cloistered
courtyard. The huge
opulent reception has
frescoes, columns and
vaults, and the 118
spacious bedrooms are
stylish.
www.fourseasons.com/milan
✉ Via Gesù 6/8, 21021 ☎ 02
770 88; fax 02 7708 5000
Ⓜ Montenapoleone

GRAND HOTEL DE
MILAN

The Grand has an
enviable position, right
next door to La Scala.
For 150 years the Grand
has opened its doors to
royals and celebrities.
The hotel oozes
distinction, with staff
buzzing around the
ornate foyer catering to
guests' every need. The
77 rooms have period
decoration, yet the
hotel's facilities are
firmly 21st century.
www.grandhoteletdemilan.it
✉ Via Manzoni 29, 20121
☎ 02 723 141; fax 02 8646
0861 Ⓜ Montenapoleone

THE GRAY

Facing the renowned
Galleria, this stylish
hotel is minimalist
design at its best: dim
lighting and metallic
decoration with a splash
of red. Framed prints
and modern lights
enhance the 21 rooms,
all with the latest mod
cons including DVDs
and hydro tubs.
www.hotelgray.com
✉ Via San Raffaele 6, 20121
☎ 02 720 8951; fax 02 866
526 Ⓜ Duomo

HERMITAGE

A refined hotel out
near the Cimitero
Monumentale with 131
bright, spacious rooms,
all furnished in dark
wood. Restaurant Il
Sambuco is said to be
one of the best in Milan
(► 64).
www.monrifhotels.it
✉ Via Messina 10, 20154
☎ 02 318 170; fax 02 3310
7399 Ⓜ Moscova

PRINCIPE DI SAVOIA

Meticulous gardens
leading up to a majestic
white façade give an
indication of the
sumptuous interior you
are about to enter. With
a 1930s feel, the rooms
are adorned with
antiques, marble and
luxury carpets. The 404
bedrooms are a generous
size. Indoor pool and
health suite.
www.hotelprincipedisavoia.com
✉ Piazza della Repubblica 17,
20124 ☎ 02 62301; fax 02
659 5838 Ⓜ Repubblica

SHERATON DIANA
MAJESTIC

Set in pretty gardens,
close to Milan's main
shopping area, this art
deco hotel is the place to
be seen; it is popular
during fashion shows
with models and
journalists. The circular
foyer has leather
armchairs and handsome
period furniture, and the
107 Imperial-style rooms
have elegant marble
bathrooms.
www.sheraton.com
/dianamajestic
✉ Viale Piave 42, 20129
☎ 02 20581; fax 02 2058
2058 Ⓜ Porta Venezia

Mid-Range Hotels

ANTICA LOCANDA SOLFERINO
Tucked away in a quiet cobbled street, this delightful old-fashioned *pensione* is very friendly. The simple but spacious rooms, decorated with antiques and chintz curtains, have pretty balconies. There are only 11 rooms, so book in advance.
✉ Via Castelfidardo 2, 20121
☎ 02 657 0129
Ⓜ Moscova

CAVOUR
In an ideal spot between La Scala and the Giardini Pubblici, this friendly hotel's 113 large rooms are decorated in cream with light-wood panelling and have satellite TV and air conditioning.
www.hotelcavour.it
✉ Via Fatebenefratelli 21, 20121 ☎ 02 620 001; fax 02 659 2263 Ⓜ Turati

KING
Housed in a lovely palazzo in a lively central location, this pleasant hotel has an opulent lobby, 48 comfortable rooms and courteous staff.
www.hotelkingmilano.com
✉ Via Corso Magenta 19, 20123
☎ 02 874 432; fax 02 8901 0798 Ⓜ Cadorna

MANZONI
Although this slightly old-fashioned hotel looks out of place among the designer boutiques of Quad d'Oro, its 52 sombre rooms generate a calming feel and the staff are warm and friendly.

www.hotelmanzoni.com
✉ Via Santo Spirito 20, 20121
☎ 02 7600 5700;
fax 02 784 212
Ⓜ Montenapoleone

HOTEL MICHELANGELO
Convenient for transport to Milan's two major airports as Stazione Centrale is visible from the hotel. Many of the 300 bedrooms have a Jacuzzi and other mod cons all surrounded by a gleaming wooden finish.
www.milanhotel.it
✉ Via Scarlatti 33, 20124
☎ 02 67551; fax 02 669 4232
Ⓜ Centrale FS

REGINA
A charming 18th-century mansion adorned with antique furniture and paintings. The 43 rooms have an old-fashioned appeal with parquet floors and large rugs. Near the Navigli canals. Pretty garden.
www.hotelregina.it
✉ Via Cesare Correnti 13, 20123 ☎ 02 5810 6913; fax 02 5810 7033
Ⓜ Missori

SPADARI AL DUOMO
A small hotel with contemporary art and sculpture displayed against vivid blue decoration. The 39 spacious bedrooms have designer furniture and each has a Jacuzzi. No restaurant, but snacks are served. A few steps from Teatro alla Scala.
www.spadarihotel.com
✉ Via Spadari 11, 20123
☎ 02 7200 2371; fax 02 286 1184 Ⓜ Duomo

PRICES AND RESERVATIONS
Italian hotels charge for the room not for each person. The price, by law, should be displayed in the room itself and may or may not include breakfast. Prices for different rooms often vary within a hotel, so if a room is too expensive be sure to ask if another is available for less (you may well be shown the most expensive first). Single rooms are in short supply and can cost nearly as much as a double room. Hotels in Milan are expensive, but they are generally of a good standard. It is best to book well in advance, particularly if there is a fashion show or trade fair taking place at the time.

Budget Hotels

SHOWER OR BATH?

Most hotel rooms in Milan have a private bathroom—unless your hotel is exceptionally basic—which will normally contain a sink, flush toilet, bidet and bath or shower. In much of Italy, showers are far more common than baths, owing to the scarcity and expense of water. You will notice a cord in the bathroom: This is a legal requirement for emergencies and summons help when pulled.

GRITTI

Close to the Duomo in a quiet square, this hotel has a very pleasant atmosphere. Its 48 rooms are well equipped, all with a bath and shower, mini-bar, and hairdryer.
✉ Piazza Santa Maria Beltrade 4, 20123 ☎ 02 801 056; fax 02 8901 0999
🚇 Duomo

LONDON HOTEL

You get a warm welcome at this central hotel, where the comfy lounge, decked with floral arrangements, is a popular place to gather. Overlooking a tranquil back street, the 30 large rooms are spartan and slightly dated.
✉ Via Rovello 3, 20121 ☎ 02 7202 0166; fax 02 805 7037
🚇 Cairoli

NUOVO

Good value for a central location. All 36 rooms are clean and compact and most have telephone, television and, some, a private bathroom. It can be noisy at night.
✉ Piazza Beccaria Cesare 6, 20122 ☎ 02 8646 4444; fax 02 7200 1752
🚇 San Babila

ROVELLO

Intimate hotel with just 10 rooms midway between the Duomo and Parco Sempione. Full of character, the rooms have wooden floors and beams, and overlook a courtyard.
www.hotel-rovello.it
✉ Via Rovello 18, 20121 ☎ 02 8646 4654; fax 02 8699 6314 🚇 Cairoli

SAN FRANCISCO

This family-run hotel close to Giardini Pubblici has 31 simple rooms and a small, beautiful garden. Welcoming staff.
www.hotel-sanfrancisco.it
✉ Viale Lombardia 55, 20131 ☎ 02 236 0302; fax 02 2668 0379 🚇 Porta Venezia

SPERONARI

A few minutes' walk from Galleria Vittorio Emanuele. The 24 rooms are small and basic but clean and tidy—some have a private bathroom. During trade fairs the hotel fills up with business guests.
✉ Via Speronari 4, 20123 ☎ 02 8646 1125; fax 02 7200 3178 🚇 Duomo

VECCHIA MILANO

In a peaceful street just off Via Torino, this charming hotel has an air of Italian antiquity. The 43 spacious rooms have old-fashioned features such as period taps and ancient portraits.
✉ Via Borromei 4, 20123 ☎ 02 875 042; fax 02 8645 4292 🚇 Duomo

HOTEL VERONA

Near Stazione Centrale, Hotel Verona makes a good-value base for exploring Milan. The 29 small, whitewashed rooms are spartan, but have televisions and phones—some have a private bathroom.
✉ Via Carlo Tenca Carlo 12, 20124 ☎ 02 6698 3091; fax 02 6698 7236
🚇 Repubblica

MILAN
travel facts

ESSENTIAL FACTS

Customs regulations

- EU nationals do not have to declare goods imported for their personal use.
- The limits for non-EU visitors are 200 cigarettes or 100 small cigars or 250g of tobacco; 1 litre of alcohol (over 22 per cent alcohol) or 2 litres of fortified wine; 50g of perfume.

Electricity

- Voltage is 220 volts and sockets take two round pins.

Etiquette

- Make the effort to speak some Italian; it will be appreciated.
- Shake hands on introduction and on leaving; once you know people better you can replace this with a kiss on each cheek.
- Use the polite form of 'you', *lei*, unless the other person uses *tu*.
- Always greet people with *buon giorno* (good morning) before lunch, and *buona sera* (good afternoon/evening) afterwards. Say *arrivederci* when leaving.
- Italians do not approve of getting drunk in public.
- Smoking is common everywhere.

Lavatories

- Expect to pay about 25c for lavatories; those away from the main tourist areas are usually free.
- There are public lavatories in the main railway station and larger museums, but otherwise they are rare in Milan.
- Most bars and cafés have lavatories, and they usually allow anybody to use them (although it's polite to have at least a drink).
- Carry your own toilet paper or a packet of tissues.

Money and credit cards

- Credit cards are widely accepted.
- Most banks have ATMs.

National holidays

- 1 Jan: New Year's Day
- 6 Jan: Epiphany
- Easter Sunday
- Easter Monday
- 25 Apr: Liberation Day
- 1 May: Labour Day
- 15 Aug: Assumption
- 1 Nov: All Saints' Day
- 8 Dec: Immaculate Conception
- 25 Dec: Christmas Day
- 26 Dec: St. Stephen's Day

- Most places of interest close on New Year's Day, 1 May and Christmas, while others close on all public holidays.

Opening times

- Banks: Mon–Fri 8.30–1.30, 3–4.
- Post offices: Mon–Fri 8.30–1.50 Sat 8–12. The main city post offices stay open at lunchtime and close at 7.
- Shops: normally 9.30–1, 3.30–7.30.
- Museums: see individual entries.
- Churches: 7 or 8–12.30, 3 or 4–7.30. Main tourist attractions often stay open longer. No two are the same.

Student travellers

- Bring an ISIC card to get reductions on museum entry fees.
- If you intend to stay at youth hostels, get a youth hostel card before leaving for Italy.

Tourist information office

- Principal tourist office Via Marconi 1, ☎ 02 7252 4301, fax 02 7252 4350; www.milanoinfotourist.com ⓘ Mon–Sat 8.45–1, 2–6; Sun & hols 9–1, 2–8.

- Stazione Centrale, First Floor,
  ☎ 02 7252 4360 ◉ Mon–Sat 9–6,
  Sun & hols 9–1, 2–8.

Women travellers

- Women are generally safe
  travelling alone in Milan.
- After dark avoid Parco Sempione,
  the railway station and poorly lit
  streets away from the middle of
  the city.

GETTING AROUND

Buses and trams

- Buses and trams are very efficient
  and run approximately every ten
  minutes. They can get very
  crowded, especially during rush
  hour, so take care of your
  belongings. Bus and tram stops
  have a yellow sign displaying the
  route and a timetable. All buses
  and trams in Milan are orange
  except for the tourist trams,
  which are green and are one of
  the best ways of seeing the city.

Scooters, mopeds and bicycles

- Even experienced riders or
  cyclists should be careful if using
  this mode of transport on Milan's
  congested roads. There are
  several places in the city that hire
  these forms of transport: try
  Bianco Blu (✉ Via Gallarate 33
  ☎ 02 3082 2430;
  www.biancolblu.com) for scooters
  and mopeds; AWS (✉ Via Ponte
  Seveso 33 ☎ 02 6707 2145) for
  bicycles.

Walking

- Walking is the best way to get
  around Milan, but do beware
  of chaotic traffic when crossing
  the road.
- For more transport information
  (► 6–7).

MEDIA & COMMUNICATIONS

Newspapers

- The daily city newspaper, *Il
  Corrière*, includes listings for
  theatre, music and cinema. Other
  Italian dailies, *La Repubblica* and
  Corriere della Sera, produce
  weekly supplements with up-to-
  date listings of cultural events in
  the city. The tourist office has two
  free magazines: *Milano è Milano*,
  in English, giving information on
  all aspects of tourism (practical
  and attractions) within the city,
  and *Mese Milano* with listings of
  what's on.
- Foreign newspapers can usually
  be bought after about 2.30 on the
  day of issue from booths (*edicole*)
  in the city. European editions of
  the *Financial Times*, *USA Today*
  and *International Herald Tribune*
  are also available.

Post offices

- Main post office ✉ Via Cordusio
  4 ☎ 02 7248 2126 ◉ Mon–Fri
  8–7, Sat 9.30–1.
- There is another big post office at
  the Central Railway Station
  ✉ Via Sammartini ☎ 02 673 951
  Mon–Fri 8–7, Sat 8.30–12.30.
- You can buy stamps (*francobolli*)
  from post offices or from
  tobacconists displaying a white
  T sign on a dark background.
- Post boxes are small, red and
  marked *Poste* or *Lettere*. The slot
  on the left is for addresses within
  the city and the slot on the right
  is for other destinations.

Telephones

- There are few telephone centres
  in the city: Galleria Vittorio
  Emanuele II ◉ Daily
  8am–9.30pm; Central Railway
  Station ◉ Daily 9am–9.30pm.

- Phone cards (*carta*, *scheda* or *tessera telefonica*) are the most practical way to use a public phone as few public telephones take coins.
- Directory Enquiries ☎ 12.
- International directory enquiries ☎ 176.
- International operator ☎ 170; you can make reverse charge international calls by dialling ☎ 17200 followed by your country code (which will give you the operator).
- Cheap rate is all day Sunday and 9pm–8am (national) on other days; 10pm–8am (international).
- To call Italy from the UK, dial 00 followed by 39 (the code for Italy) then the number. To call the UK from Italy dial 00 44 then drop the first zero from the area code.
- To call Italy from the US dial 011 followed by 39. To call the US from Italy dial 00 1.
- Milan's area code (02) must be dialled even if you are calling from within the city.

EMERGENCIES

Consulates
- British Consulate ✉ Via San Paulo 7 ☎ 02 723 001 🕐 Mon–Fri 9.15–12.15, 2.30–4.30.
- US Consulate ✉ Via Principe Amedeo 2/10 ☎ 02 290 351 🕐 Mon–Fri 8.30–5.30.

Emergency telephone numbers
- Police ☎ 113.
- Police (Carabinieri) ☎ 112.
- Police headquarters (for foreigners and passport office) ✉ Via Montebello 26 ☎ 02 62261.
- Fire ☎ 115.
- Ambulance ☎ 118.

- Breakdown service Automobile Club di Milano (ACI) ☎ 116.

Lost property
- Council lost property office ✉ Via Friuli 30 ☎ 02 8845 3907/8 🕐 Mon–Fri 8.30–4.
- Central railway left luggage office ✉ Stazione Centrale (first floor of Galleria Partenze) ☎ 02 6371 2667 🕐 Daily 6am–1am.
- Report losses of passports to the police.

Medicines and medical treatment
- Medical emergencies ☎ 118 or go to the *Pronto Soccorso* (casualty department or emergency room) of the nearest hospital .
- Poison Antidote Centre ☎ 02 6610 1029.
- Pharmacies are indicated by a large green or red cross.
- There is a free emergency number for your nearest pharmacy ☎ 800 801 185. 24-hour pharmacy: Farmacia della Stazione Centrale ☎ 02 669 0935.
- There are several night pharmacies including those located in: Piazza Duomo 21 ☎ 02 287 8668; Via Boccaccio 26 ☎ 02 469 5281; Corso Magenta ☎ 02 4800 6772.

Sensible precautions
- Take care of wallets, handbags and backpacks as pickpockets target tourists. Be especially careful around train stations, on public transport and in crowded areas.
- Only carry what you need for the day and consider making use of safe deposit facilities in your hotel.
- Keep the receipts and numbers of your traveller's cheques

separately from the traveller's cheques.
• Keep a copy of the information page of your passport.
• List the numbers and expiry dates of your credit cards and keep the list separately.
• If a theft occurs, make a statement (*denuncia*) at a police station within 24 hours if you wish to make an insurance claim.

LANGUAGE

• Italian pronunciation is totally consistent. Cs and gs are hard when they are followed by an a, o or u (as in 'cat' and 'got'), and soft if followed by an e or an i (as in 'child' or 'geranium').
• The Tuscans often pronounce their cs and chs as hs.

Useful words and phrases
good morning buon giorno
good afternoon/good evening buona sera
good night buona notte
hello/goodbye (informal) ciao
goodbye (informal) arrivederci
please per favore
thank you grazie
you're welcome prego
how are you? come sta/stai?
I'm fine sto bene
I'm sorry mi dispiace
excuse me/I beg your pardon scusi/scusa
excuse me (in a crowd) permesso

Basic vocabulary
yes sì
no no
I do not understand non ho capito
left sinistra
right destra
entrance entrata
exit uscita
open aperto
closed chiuso

good buono
bad cattivo
big grande
small piccolo
with con
without senza
more più
less meno
near vicino
far lontano
hot caldo
cold freddo
here qui/qua
there là/li
today oggi
tomorrow domani
yesterday ieri
how much is it? quant'è?
when? quando?
do you have …? avete…?

Emergencies
help! aiuto!
where is the nearest telephone? dov'è il telefono più vicino?
there has been an accident c'è stato un incidente
call the police chiamate la polizia
call a doctor/an ambulance chiamate un medico/un'ambulanza
first aid pronto soccorso
where is the nearest hospital? dov'è l'ospedale più vicino?

Numbers
one uno, una
two due
three tre
four quattro
five cinque
six sei
seven sette
eight otto
nine nove
ten dieci
twenty venti
fifty cinquanta
one hundred cento
one thousand mille

Index

95

Citypack
milan's 25 best

AUTHORS *Jackie Staddon and Hilary Weston*
COVER DESIGN *Tigist Getachew, Fabrizio La Rocca*

ISBN 13: 978-1-4000-1516-0
ISBN 10: 1-4000-1516-2

FIRST EDITION

ACKNOWLEDGMENTS
The Automobile Association would like to thank the following photographers, libraries and associations for their assistance in the preparation of this title.
Marka 24cr, 29, 30t, 30c, 37, 38t, 45, 51t, 54, 55, 56, 59, 60; Scala Archives 36; Stockbyte 5; Stock Italia/Alamy 39; World Pictures 33, 40, 42, 49.
The remaining pictures are held in the Association's own library (AA WORLD TRAVEL LIBRARY) and were taken by Max Jourdan, with the exception of 16cl which was taken by Pete Bennett.

IMPORTANT TIP
Time inevitably brings changes, so always confirm prices, travel facts, and other perishable information when it matters. Although Fodor's cannot accept responsibility for errors, you can use this guide in the confidence that we have taken every care to ensure its accuracy.

SPECIAL SALES
This book is available for special discounts for bulk purchases for sales promotions or premiums. Special editions, including personalized covers, excerpts of existing books, and corporate imprints, can be created in large quantities for special needs. For more information, write to Special Markets/Premium Sales, 1745 Broadway, MD 6-2, New York, NY 10019 or e-mail specialmarkets@randomhouse.com.

Color separation by Daylight Colour Art Pte Ltd., Singapore
Manufactured by Hang Tai D&P Limited, Hong Kong.
10 9 8 7 6 5 4 3 2

A02971
Maps in this title produced from mapping © MAIRDUMONT/Falk Verlag 2006
Fold out map © MAIRDUMONT/ Falk Verlag 2006

TITLES IN THE CITYPACK SERIES
• Amsterdam • Bangkok • Barcelona • Beijing • Berlin • Boston • Brussels & Bruges •
• Chicago • Dublin • Florence • Hong Kong • Lisbon • London • Los Angeles • Madrid •
• Melbourne • Miami • Milan • Montréal • Munich • Naples • New York City • Paris •
• Prague • Rome • San Francisco • Seattle • Shanghai • Singapore • Sydney • Tokyo •
• Toronto • Venice • Vienna • Washington D. C. •